RIVER FLOW

BOOKS BY DAVID WHYTE

POETRY

Songs for Coming Home
Where Many Rivers Meet
Fire in the Earth
The House of Belonging
Everything is Waiting for You
Pilgrim
The Sea in You: Twenty Poems of Requited and Unrequited Love
The Bell and The Blackbird

PROSE

The Heart Aroused:
Poetry and the Preservation of the Soul
in Corporate America

Crossing the Unknown Sea:
Work as a Pilgrimage of Identity

The Three Marriages:
Reimagining Work, Self & Relationship

Consolations:
The Solace, Nourishment and Underlying Meaning of Everyday Words

RIVER FLOW

REVISED EDITION

New & Selected Poems
by DAVID WHYTE

20  19

MANY RIVERS PRESS
LANGLEY, WASHINGTON

First published in 2007
by Many Rivers Press
P.O. Box 868
Langley, WA 98260
U.S.A.

A catalog record for this book
is available from the Library of Congress.

Library of Congress Control Number: 2006937553

ISBN-13: 978-1-932887-27-3
ISBN-10: 1-932887-27-3

ISBN-13: 978-1-932887-28-0
ISBN-10: 1-932887-28-0

First printing 2012
Second printing 2014
Third printing 2015
Fourth printing 2016
Fifth printing 2017
Sixth printing 2018
Seventh printing 2019

For
Jayne and Tracy,
my two extraordinary
and saintly sisters,
whose faith and compassion
were tested
and not found wanting,
to the very end.

RIVER FLOW CONTENTS

I. HOME

3	Coming Back to the House	*Songs for Coming Home*
4	Home	*Songs for Coming Home*
6	The House of Belonging	*The House of Belonging*
9	At Home	*The House of Belonging*
12	It Happens to Those Who Live Alone	*The House of Belonging*
15	Winter Child	*The House of Belonging*
16	The Winter of Listening	*The House of Belonging*

II. MOMENTS

23	Horses Moving on the Snow	*Songs for Coming Home*
24	Light Over Water	*Songs for Coming Home*
25	The Wildflower	*Songs for Coming Home*
26	Owl Calls	*Where Many Rivers Meet*
27	Easter Morning in Wales	*Where Many Rivers Meet*
28	Seen from Above	*Where Many Rivers Meet*

III. REVELATION

31	The Opening of Eyes	*Songs for Coming Home*
32	The Song of the Lark	*Songs for Coming Home*
33	Up On the Hill's Back	*Songs for Coming Home*
34	Fire in the Earth	*Fire in the Earth*
35	Traveling to London	*Fire in the Earth*
38	Unutterable Name	*Fire in the Earth*
43	Sitting Zen	*Fire in the Earth*
44	Open	*Fire in the Earth*
45	We Shall Not be Here	*Fire in the Earth*
46	Death Waits	*Fire in the Earth*
48	Midsummer Prayer	*Fire in the Earth*
50	The Half Turn of Your Face	*Fire in the Earth*
52	Sometimes	*Everything is Waiting For You*

RIVER FLOW CONTENTS *(continued)*

54	When the Wind Flows	*Everything is Waiting For You*
56	The Thicket	*Everything is Waiting For You*
59	Sligo Glen: Walking out of Silence	*Everything is Waiting For You*
62	The Bell Ringer	*Everything is Waiting For You*
67	Mortality My Mistress	*New Poems*
70	Waiting to Go On	*New Poems*
75	Arrivals	*New Poems*
78	The Hazel Wood	*New Poems*
81	Who Made The Stars?	*New Poems*

IV. THE WELL

93	Inside	*Songs for Coming Home*
94	Faith	*Where Many Rivers Meet*
95	The Well of Grief	*Where Many Rivers Meet*
96	Forgive	*Everything is Waiting For You*
97	Threshold	*Everything is Waiting For You*
99	Fishing	*Everything is Waiting For You*
101	The Shell	*Everything is Waiting For You*
104	Farewell Letter	*Everything is Waiting For You*
106	Looking	*Everything is Waiting For You*
108	Dance Night in Waterford City	*Everything is Waiting For You*
112	Ancestral	*New Poems*
114	Stepping Stones	*New Poems*
117	Tempus Omnia Revelat	*New Poems*

V. WRITING

121	Seven Steps for Coming Home	*Songs for Coming Home*
122	Muse	*Where Many Rivers Meet*
123	The Task at Hand	*Where Many Rivers Meet*
124	One Day	*Where Many Rivers Meet*

RIVER FLOW CONTENTS *(continued)*

125	The Painter's Hand	*Fire in the Earth*
128	The Poet	*Fire in the Earth*
130	The Body in Full Presence	*Fire in the Earth*
131	No One Told Me	*Fire in the Earth*
132	Four Horses	*The House of Belonging*
135	This Poem Belongs to You	*The House of Belonging*
136	The Lightest Touch	*Everything is Waiting For You*
137	My Poetry	*Everything is Waiting For You*
139	Mariner	*Everything is Waiting For You*

VI. REMEMBER

145	Where Many Rivers Meet	*Where Many Rivers Meet*
146	Song For the Salmon	*Where Many Rivers Meet*
147	Vision on the Hills	*Where Many Rivers Meet*
149	Time Left Alone	*Where Many Rivers Meet*
151	What it Means to be Free	*Fire in the Earth*
152	Horse in Landscape: Franz Marc	*Fire in the Earth*
154	You Darkness *Rilke*	*Fire in the Earth*
155	The Well of Stars	*The House of Belonging*
158	Once Round the Moon	*Everything is Waiting For You*
161	Learning To Walk	*New Poems*
165	Remember	*New Poems*
167	Apology	*New Poems*

VII. EXILE

171	What is it Like?	*Where Many Rivers Meet*
172	Actaeon Tells All	*Where Many Rivers Meet*
173	John Clare's Madness	*Where Many Rivers Meet*
175	This Time	*Fire in the Earth*
178	Never Enough	*Fire in the Earth*
179	Second Birth	*Fire in the Earth*
180	New Year Prayer	*New Poems*

RIVER FLOW CONTENTS *(continued)*

VIII. THE CONSEQUENCE OF LOVE

185	Pisac, Peru	*Where Many Rivers Meet*
186	Huaras	*Where Many Rivers Meet*
188	Ayacucho	*Where Many Rivers Meet*
190	Cuzco	*Where Many Rivers Meet*
192	Macchu Picchu	*Where Many Rivers Meet*
194	In a Moment of Madness, a Dublin Poet Thinks of an Old Love	*Where Many Rivers Meet*
195	The Hawthorn	*The House of Belonging*
198	The Truelove	*The House of Belonging*
201	Living Together	*Everything is Waiting For You*
202	Marriage	*Everything is Waiting For You*
204	The Poet as Husband	*Everything is Waiting For You*
205	The Vows at Glencolmcille	*Everything is Waiting For You*

IX. SONS & DAUGHTERS

213	First Steps in Hawkshead Churchyard	*Where Many Rivers Meet*
214	Brendan	*The House of Belonging*
217	My Daughter Asleep	*New Poems*

X. THE VOICE

225	The Soul Lives Contented	*Fire in the Earth*
226	Revelation Must be Terrible	*Fire in the Earth*
228	The Fire in the Song	*Fire in the Earth*
230	The Sound of the Wild	*Fire in the Earth*

XI. FROM THE KAYAK

239	Kayak I	*Songs for Coming Home*
240	Kayak IV	*Songs for Coming Home*
241	Kayak VI	*Songs for Coming Home*

RIVER FLOW CONTENTS *(continued)*

243	Out On the Ocean	*Songs for Coming Home*
245	Watching the Sun Go Down	*Where Many Rivers Meet*
246	Setting out at Dusk	*Where Many Rivers Meet*
247	Ten Years Later	*The House of Belonging*

XII. ALBION

251	There are Those	*Where Many Rivers Meet*
252	Cotswold	*Where Many Rivers Meet*
254	Hartshead	*Where Many Rivers Meet*
256	Yorkshire	*The House of Belonging*

XIII. IRELAND

265	Hands Across the Water	*Where Many Rivers Meet*
267	Return	*Where Many Rivers Meet*
268	Spiddal Harbour 1976	*Where Many Rivers Meet*
269	Seeking out Time	*Where Many Rivers Meet*
271	Poem in Praise of The Trinity Harp	*Where Many Rivers Meet*
272	The Horse Whisperer	*The House of Belonging*
276	Tiananmen	*The House of Belonging*
281	The All of It	*New Poems*
283	Dun Aengus	*New Poems*
285	The Seven Streams	*New Poems*
286	Mameen	*New Poems*
287	Tobar Phadraic	*New Poems*
288	Coleman's Bed	*New Poems*

XIV. HIMALAYA

293	Muktinath	*Where Many Rivers Meet*
295	Tilicho Lake	*Where Many Rivers Meet*
296	The Faces at Braga	*Where Many Rivers Meet*
299	Dreaming at Braga	*Where Many Rivers Meet*
300	Bed Bugs in Kagbeni	*Where Many Rivers Meet*

RIVER FLOW CONTENTS *(continued)*

301	A Woman's Voice	*Where Many Rivers Meet*
302	This Poem a Prayer Flag	*Fire in the Earth*
303	Takstang	*Fire in the Earth*
305	The Old Interior Angel	*Fire in the Earth*
308	Statue of Buddha	*Fire in the Earth*
309	Statue of Shiva	*Fire in the Earth*

XV. THOSE I KNOW AND HAVE KNOWN

313	News of Death	*Where Many Rivers Meet*
314	Tan-y-Garth	*Where Many Rivers Meet*
316	Edward	*The House of Belonging*
321	Dougie	*The House of Belonging*
325	Firelight and Memory	*Everything is Waiting For You*
331	True	*Everything is Waiting For You*
334	Looking out from Clare	*Everything is Waiting For You*
337	Richard	*Everything is Waiting For You*
339	The Fox	*Everything is Waiting For You*
340	Summer Reading	*New Poems*

XVI. ADMONITIONS

345	Self-Portrait	*Fire in the Earth*
346	Sweet Darkness	*The House of Belonging*
347	All the True Vows	*The House of Belonging*
349	What to Remember When Waking	*The House of Belonging*
352	The Journey	*The House of Belonging*
354	Working Together	*The House of Belonging*
356	Loaves and Fishes	*The House of Belonging*
357	The New Nobility	*Everything is Waiting For You*
359	Everything is Waiting For You	*Everything is Waiting For You*
360	Start Close In	*New Poems*
362	No Path	*New Poems*

365	Index of Poem Titles
370	Index of First Lines

CHRONOLOGICAL CONTENTS

New and Selected Poems

Songs for Coming Home (1984-86)

3	Coming Back to the House
32	The Song of the Lark
23	Horses Moving On The Snow
24	Light Over Water
93	Inside
33	Up on The Hill's Back
31	The Opening of Eyes
25	The Wildflower
239	Kayak I
240	Kayak IV
241	Kayak VI
243	Out on the Ocean
4	Home
121	Seven Steps for Coming Home

Where Many Rivers Meet (1990)

94	Faith
122	Muse
145	Where Many Rivers Meet
149	Time Left Alone
245	Watching the Sun Go Down
246	Setting out at Dusk
146	Song for the Salmon
293	Muktinath
295	Tilicho Lake
296	The Faces at Braga
299	Dreaming at Braga
300	Bed Bugs in Kagbeni
301	A Woman's Voice
95	The Well of Grief
171	What is it Like?
172	Actaeon tells All
173	John Clare's Madness
313	News of Death

147	Vision on the Hills
185	Pisac, Peru
186	Huaras
188	Ayacucho
190	Cuzco
192	Macchu Picchu
251	There are Those
213	First Steps in Hawkshead Churchyard
26	Owl Calls
252	Cotswold
254	Hartshead
314	Tan-y-Garth
27	Easter Morning In Wales
265	Hands across the Water
267	Return
268	Spiddal Harbour 1976
269	Seeking out Time
271	Poem in Praise of the Trinity Harp
28	Seen from Above
123	The Task at Hand
124	One Day

Fire in the Earth *(1992)*

34	Fire in the Earth
151	What it Means to be Free
345	Self-Portrait
35	Traveling to London
125	The Painter's Hand
175	This Time
178	Never Enough
154	You Darkness
225	The Soul Lives Contented
226	Revelation Must be Terrible
228	The Fire in the Song
230	The Sound of the Wild
128	The Poet
130	The Body in Full Presence
131	No One Told Me
152	Horse in Landscape: Franz Marc

CHRONOLOGICAL CONTENTS *(continued)*

179   Second Birth
38   Unutterable Name
43   Sitting Zen
44   Open
45   We Shall not be Here
46   Death Waits
48   Midsummer Prayer
50   The Half Turn of Your Face
302   This Poem a Prayer Flag
303   Takstang
305   The Old Interior Angel
308   Statue of Buddha
309   Statue of Shiva

The House of Belonging   (1997)

6   The House of Belonging
9   At Home
12   It Happens to those Who Live Alone
15   Winter Child
346   Sweet Darkness
347   All the True Vows
349   What to Remember When Waking
16   The Winter of Listening
155   The Well of Stars
352   The Journey
256   Yorkshire
247   Ten Years Later
132   Four Horses
273   The Horse Whisperer
276   Tiananmen
214   Brendan
316   Edward
321   Dougie
195   The Hawthorn
354   Working Together
356   Loaves and Fishes
135   This Poem Belongs To You
198   The Truelove

Everything is Waiting For You (2003)

136	The Lightest Touch
52	Sometimes
359	Everything is Waiting for You
357	The New Nobility
137	My Poetry
96	Forgive
97	Threshold
99	Fishing
32	The Shell
104	Farewell Letter
158	Once Round the Moon
106	Looking
108	Dance Night in Waterford City
325	Firelight and Memory
331	True
334	Looking out from Clare
337	Richard
201	Living Together
202	Marriage
204	The Poet as Husband
205	The Vows at Glencolmcille
339	The Fox
54	When the Wind Flows
56	The Thicket
139	Mariner
59	Sligo Glen: Walking out of Silence
62	The Bell Ringer

CHRONOLOGICAL CONTENTS *(continued)*

New (2007)

360	Start close In
362	No Path
161	Learning to Walk
340	Summer Reading
67	Mortality My Mistress
112	Ancestral
114	Stepping Stones
217	My Daughter Asleep
180	New Year Prayer
70	Waiting to Go On
281	The All of It
75	Arrivals
165	Remember
167	Apology
81	Who Made the Stars?
78	The Hazel Wood
283	Dun Aengus
285	The Seven Streams
286	Mameen
287	Tobar Phadraic
288	Coleman's Bed
117	Tempus Omnia Revelat
365	Index of Poem Titles
370	Index of First Lines

[I]
HOME

COMING BACK TO THE HOUSE

COMING BACK TO THE HOUSE I lean down into the snow
and pick it up with both hands, where it shivers like a small
animal stirred by the cold breeze: — a black leaf, torn in
the center, a swirly criss-cross of dark and striated white put
there with startling urgency. One gaping hole shows me how
a cut edge crinkles. There is a small curve at one end where
a piece of grass sticks to it. In my closing hands it makes a
sound like parchment, but nothing is written. It is cut, torn
and fragile, and balances on only a thin line of its stem
. . . a fallen leaf three months after even the last of summer,
how dark it seems against the snow! Entering the house I
walk over to the table and put it down, and touching
one end I make the leaf rock. A cradle for quiet
thoughts as night draws close.

HOME

Home:
A long road on the raven coast
on the roof
two kayaks
bend through the warm air
a resonant hum
in their tight ropes
sings in the evening light.

Headlights switched on
as the car dips through hollows
and the colors deepen.

We all speak together
or are silent.

At Deception Pass
the water ripples
under our bellies
and our souls leap
in a sudden feeling
to swim north
with salmon eyes
nudging between islands.

The western sky warms
and we ease through the land

two lights
in the slowly moving darkness

outside
dew gathers on dry branches

my wife turns
speaks to me
reminds me of a crossing
yesterday
on a calm sea
and we laugh in the dark interior
of the car

with two friends fallen asleep
in the back
heading south through the
dark night
and home.

THE HOUSE OF BELONGING

I awoke
this morning
in the gold light
turning this way
and that

thinking for
a moment
it was one
day
like any other.

But
the veil had gone
from my
darkened heart
and
I thought

it must have been the quiet
candlelight
that filled my room,

it must have been
the first
easy rhythm
with which I breathed
myself to sleep,

it must have been
the prayer I said
speaking to the otherness
of the night.

And
I thought
this is the good day
you could
meet your love,

this is the gray day
someone close
to you could die.

This is the day
you realize
how easily the thread
is broken
between this world
and the next

and I found myself
sitting up
in the quiet pathway
of light,

the tawny
close grained cedar
burning round
me like fire
and all the angels of this housely
heaven ascending
through the first
roof of light
the sun has made.

This is the bright home
in which I live,
this is where
I ask
my friends
to come,
this is where I want
to love all the things
it has taken me so long
to learn to love.

This is the temple
of my adult aloneness
and I belong
to that aloneness
as I belong to my life.

There is no house
like the house of belonging.

AT HOME

At home amidst
the bees
wandering
the garden
in the summer
light
the sky
a broad roof
for the house
of contentment
where I wish
to
live forever
in the eternity
of my own
fleeting
and momentary
happiness.

I walk toward
the kitchen
door as if walking
toward the
door of a recognized
heaven

and see the
simplicity
of shelves and
the blue dishes
and the
vaporing

steam rising
from the kettle
that called me in.

Not just this
aromatic cup
from which to drink
but the flavor
of a life made whole
and lovely
through the
imagination
seeking its way.

Not just this
house around me
but the arms
of a fierce
but healing world.

Not just this line
I write
but the
innocence
of an earned
forgiveness
flowing again
through hands
made new with
writing.

And a man
with no company
but his house,
his garden,
and his own
well peopled solitude,

entering
the silences
and chambers
of the heart
to start again.

IT HAPPENS TO THOSE WHO LIVE ALONE

It happens to those
who live alone
that they feel sure
of visitors
when no one else
is there,

until the one day
and one particular
hour
working in the
quiet garden,

when they realize
at once,
that all along
they have been
an invitation
to everything
and every kind of trouble

and that life
happens by
to those who
inhabit
silence

like the bees
visiting
the tall mallow
on their legs of gold,
or the wasps
going from door to door
in the tall forest
of the daisies.

I have my freedom
today
because
nothing really happened

and nobody came
to see me.
Only the slow
growing of the garden
in the summer heat

and the silence of that
unborn life
making itself
known at my desk,

my hands
still
dark with the
crumbling soil
as I write
and watch

the first lines
of a new poem,
like flowers
of scarlet fire,
coming to fullness
in a new light.

WINTER CHILD

Myself at my door
like Blake
at home in his
heaven
my own heart
newly opened
by the news
and my face
turned upward
and innocent
toward them.

All the stars
like a great crowd
of creation singing

above the blessed house.

THE WINTER OF LISTENING

No one but me by the fire,
my hands burning
red in the palms while
the night wind carries
everything away outside.

All this petty worry
while the great cloak
of the sky grows dark
and intense
round every living thing.

What is precious
inside us does not
care to be known
by the mind
in ways that diminish
its presence.

What we strive for
in perfection
is not what turns us
into the lit angel
we desire.

What disturbs
and then nourishes
has everything
we need.

What we hate
in ourselves
is what we cannot know
in ourselves but
what is true to the pattern
does not need
to be explained.

Inside everyone
is a great shout of joy
waiting to be born.

Even with summer
so far off
I feel it grown in me
now and ready
to arrive in the world.

All those years
listening to those
who had
nothing to say.

All those years
forgetting
how everything
has its own voice
to make
itself heard.

All those years
forgetting
how easily
you can belong
to everything
simply by listening.

And the slow
difficulty
of remembering
how everything
is born from
an opposite
and miraculous
otherness.

Silence and winter
have led me to that
otherness.

So let this winter
of listening
be enough
for the new life
I must call my own.

We speak
only with the voices of those
we can hear ourselves
and the body has a voice
only for that portion
of the body of the world
it has learned to perceive.

And
here
in the tumult
of the night
I hear the walnut
above the child's swing
swaying
its dark limbs
in the wind
and the rain now
come to
beat against my window
and somewhere
in this cold night
of wind and stars
the first whispered
opening of
those hidden
and invisible springs
that uncoil
in the still summer air
each yet
to be imagined
rose.

[II]
MOMENTS

HORSES MOVING ON THE SNOW

In winter
through the damp grass
around the house
there are horses moving
on the snow

in the half-light
they move quickly

following the fence
until the mist takes them
      completely

and evening
is the hollow sound of hooves
in the south field.

LIGHT OVER WATER

Through the light on the upper line of water
three birds
with wings extended into the center of brightness
turn south into the channel
flicking their wings through the currents of air
to a silent horizon that empties the wind of sound.

In that noiseless wind they turn
and in the sudden gusts as they lift
the dark throats of the evening birds turn white.

THE WILDFLOWER

In the center of this wildflower
the names of things revolve like planets
and as if pulled by tides
and the gravity of deep space
the names of things move into form
through enormous distance.

Like electrons enchanted
by the atom
they show their undiscovered seas
as they revolve.

But for this dark flower
I give it the name of a hidden moon.

OWL CALLS

Late evening in Esthwaite and the half-moon rides
above a still lake of clouds. Only the white sweep
of car lights curving through hedgerows, only the mind
coming to rest in tired arms, leaning on the rough wood gate.

Across the quiet field two white owls glide
toward the wood, beneath them only the dark bulk
of cows to be heard, cropping the fresh wet grass
and the still water color sky washed above the eyes.

Then from my own lips, the first whispering of an old poem,
long memorized, each line outlined by quiet. The young boy
blowing in his fists to call the owls, baffled by silence,
uncertain, unsure of what he called.

The owl's voice returned, the long silence,
the mouth open in surprise as if to speak,
and even now I sense the first faint crawl of his skin
and shiver of cold, as in that same moment, empty of sound,
the scarlet brake-lights flare between trees and are gone.

EASTER MORNING IN WALES

A garden inside me, unknown, secret,
neglected for years,
the layers of its soil deep and thick.
Trees in the corners with branching arms
and the tangled briars like broken nets.

Sunrise through the misted orchard,
morning sun turns silver on the pointed twigs.
I have woken from the sleep of ages and I am not sure
if I am really seeing, or dreaming,
or simply astonished
walking toward sunrise
to have stumbled into the garden
where the stone was rolled from the tomb of longing.

SEEN FROM ABOVE

Seeing from a high window
the three years old boy
caught by sunlight,
peeing in the garden,
I am suddenly aware
why those small statues abound
gracing our squares and piazzas!

The form is eternal delight,
and the source of that
long golden arch of urine a blessing
of curved tummy and bended knees.

Hands clapped on bottom,
eyes concentrated somewhere
between source and target,
amazed, enraptured,
and miracle again,
the golden line between
subject and object made clear,
whose author,
transcending duality,
looks out at a world
intimately
experiencing his arrival.

[III]
REVELATION

THE OPENING OF EYES

After R. S. Thomas

That day I saw beneath dark clouds,
the passing light over the water
and I heard the voice of the world speak out,
I knew then, as I had before,
life is no passing memory of what has been
nor the remaining pages in a great book
waiting to be read.

It is the opening of eyes long closed.
It is the vision of far off things
seen for the silence they hold.
It is the heart after years
of secret conversing,
speaking out loud in the clear air.

It is Moses in the desert
fallen to his knees before the lit bush.
It is the man throwing away his shoes
as if to enter heaven
and finding himself astonished,
opened at last,
fallen in love with solid ground.

THE SONG OF THE LARK

The song begins and the eyes are lifted
but the sickle points toward the ground,
its downward curve forgotten in the song she hears,
while over the dark wood, rising or falling,
the sun lifts on cool air,
the small body of a singing lark.

The song falls, the eyes raise, the mouth opens
and her bare feet on the earth have stopped.

Whoever listens in this silence, as she listens,
will also stand opened, thoughtless, frightened
by the joy she feels, the pathway in the field
branching to a hundred more, no one has explored.

What is called in her rises from the ground
and is found in her body,
what she is given is secret even from her.

This silence is the seed in her
of everything she is
and falling through her body
to the ground from which she comes,
it finds a hidden place to grow
and rises, and flowers, in old wild places,
where the dark-edged sickle cannot go.

UP ON THE HILL'S BACK

Up on the hill's back
field lines have stopped
memories still pass the next horizon
nothing halts the age of the body walking
not the young growth of trees
nor the fallen trunk across the hill path.

When I have passed this way
the crows
will still bear down fiercely from the west
the lights wink on
and night come bringing rain
sweeping the branches down

life passes
and clouds mound darkness in the west
where the path turns
grass breaks in furrows down the hill

whoever asks of darkness
must touch the darkness in himself
whoever asks of grass
bend down in the moving stalks
and under the blades
feel the small birds shivering
waiting to rise in the morning light.

FIRE IN THE EARTH

And we know, when Moses was told,
   in the way he was told,
"Take off your shoes!" He grew pale from that simple

reminder of fire in the dusty earth.
   He never recovered
his complicated way of loving again

and was free to love in the same way
   he felt the fire licking at his heels loved him.
As if the lion earth could roar

and take him in one movement.
   Every step he took
from there was carefully placed.

Everything he said mattered as if he knew
   the constant witness of the ground
and remembered his own face in the dust

the moment before revelation.
   Since then thousands have felt
the same immobile tongue with which he tried to speak.

Like the moment you too saw, for the first time,
   your own house turned to ashes.
Everything consumed so the road could open again.

Your entire presence in your eyes
   and the world turning slowly
into a single branch of flame.

TRAVELING TO LONDON

Coleridge's eyes
belonged to the world.
The black mass
of starlings
smoking over the ridge
was his life.
No fancy this
but feverish
with their black shapes
his view
was to fly with them.
Make each word
follow each bird.
His grief accorded
directly
from what he saw
but could not speak.
Their mesmerizing dispersion
summed up the
limit of his powers.
Their protean shape
shifting through
his jolted body
held joy and chaotic
terror
as if he glimpsed
through the moving
carriage window
a portrait of himself
too terrifying to realize.

Now, the wintry
line of moor glowering
to an unnamed blue
broods beneath
an empty grey.
Now, each black speck,
scattered and reformed,
holds attention
to its gravitational
center. The turbulent
reflector of his eyes
no longer accustomed
to watching, can only
join its misted surface
of infinitely smaller
curves. Beneath,
the graph-straight line
of the moors
where imagination
equals zero,
is cut again and again
by their flight.

The flight of amazing freedoms
held in tension
by the menace
of impending chaos.

The cloud
of his own unknowing
darting this way
and that.

Like the lithe
shadow
of something deeper
suddenly revealed
in the sky.
His single vision
exploded
to a firework of doubles.

UNUTTERABLE NAME

Cross-currents and tumbling desire
of aspens in a summer wind,
shimmering in a rustle and whisper

of leaf undersides turned pale
yellow, each upper side
a trembling of bright green.

The whole frame a lit firework
of feeling where all
surfaces and shoulders of wood

and leaf touch and quiver
to the wind's
quaking unspoken desire.

Not to be lightly spoken of.
Your species name
so common on our tongue

the mind's eye forgets the continued
revelation of your kind.
A single branch, a copse, a nest of bright

copper for the dying year. All the
forests of the world
were wild wood once and proclaim

the leafy hope and snares of human paradise.
The wild wood, bramble, columbine,
the oak tree's deciduous stability of half-light.

In your branches the robin and the wren,
the crows, the rooks, the owls, the sparrow-
hawk gliding the fine speckled corridors of light.

Of all your many worlds I'll start by naming home,
this sharp evergreen night's
rough-barked verticality of totem and grey wood

lifted two hundred feet to a cold sky,
its grey clouds unseen above the world's
green turn of pine and hemlock, fir and cedar

shadowing the paddled needle beds
in their brown sleep.
Even here, Pan's mad flute wakes them all,

a scurry of chipmunks and tremulous mice,
a moment's panic before the
creaking whine of a branch lifts the hair

straight on the neck, the owl's prey screams
in discovered claws and the patient empty
darkness of the deep wood returns to quiet.

Even then, the still temple of the northern night
opening its doors to the first delicate light
and the nightjar burring at a branch edge

is nothing to the jungle's southern tumult and tropic
dark panoply of explosive sound.
In that equatorial fusion of heat and noise,

where a scream would be lost in the whistling,
cawing, shuddering, sighing
rippling, spider-monkeyed laugh and great shaking

of the canopy's jungle dark essence,
there lies that eternally moving
half-hidden, essentially frightening

forest of our own inner night. Down below,
the dream of those dark limbs turning
now feminine, now snake-like, erotically

refusing to be found, leads us down
into that glistering world-wide
treasure of wetness and wild abandon, the marsh.

The dank water's cool refusal of dryness
a sworn enemy to the clarity
our yearning demands, every footstep

filled with mud, every feeling a mere mushroom
subsumed by damp, a fever
of scents, sounds and recollection, how the bark

smells, how the frogs breathe, how the greens
seem darker still. How the faint
brushing sting of nettle feels on passing skin.

The stagnant still fullness of it all with no place
to rest, sit, camp, cook, build,
get in, get out, lie down with self or other.

The infuriating self-satisfied independent
non-human presence
of this methane-flitted, black and fiery

incandescence of wetness eschewing our praise,
resting into its own eternal wet grave
of damp hidden mischief. The damned and lovely swamp.

Not forgetting for one moment the dry desert
branches of the world's
desiccated, rough-barked, wax-leafed elders.

The pinon, chaparral, boll-weed and wind-dried
dust-loving Joshua, even the names
have a dry mouth salted by heat and smothered

by thirst. Tenacity a prize of their kind,
living patiently through the hard
baked inhospitable prison of eternal summer,

and they need, we still do not believe it,
just the one, gifted, single drop
of fecund rain swimming through red earth

to break out in a blood red, snow white
festival of still flowers.
Or a lit inextinguishable fire of perfect yellow.

All your many kinds are filled with our stories.
We know you, name you
Aspen, Rowan, Linden, Oak, and remember

Pan's stable of haunting desire,
Kevin's seat of still prayer,
Buddha's explosive clarity beneath

the Bodhi's protecting shadow of knowledge.
Christ's arms like branches
on the still sapling of longing and loss.

Your stories are our welcome night sign
of stop and rest and sky and stars
and forgotten sleep where we wake again

to find we are surrounded, embellished,
frighted, nourished,
sheltered, restored, rejected and inhabited

by – how shall I ever say your name?
Wood, trunk, branch, leaf,
boreal harmony of green in-breath,

my hands clapping, eyes opened,
mouth attempting the song
of your unspeakable gifts and grace

again and again– the full hidden
not to be said, mysterious
and unutterable name of your full breath. Tree.

SITTING ZEN

After three days of sitting
hard by the window
following grief through
the breath

like a hunter
who has tracked for days
the blood spots
of his injured prey

I came to the lake
where the deer had run
exhausted

refusing to save
its life in the
dark water

and there it fell
to ground
in our mutual
and respectful quiet

pierced
by
the pale diamond
edge of the breath's
listening
presence.

OPEN

It is a small step to remember
how life led to this
moment's hesitation.

How the door to the deeper world
opens, letting the body fall at last,
toward the few griefs it can call its own.

Oh yes, I know. Our wings catch fire
in that downward flight
and we come to earth afraid
we can never fly again.

But then we always knew
heaven would be a desperate place.
Everything you desired coming
in one fearful moment
to greet you.

Your full presence only in rest
and the love that asks nothing.
The rest where you lie down
and are no longer found at all.

WE SHALL NOT BE HERE

Heaven has been
promised
in great detail.

Beyond this silence
we shall not be here
to find it.
And that, my friend

is a great joy.

DEATH WAITS

Death waits behind the branches
refusing to show his face.

The child opens his eyes and sees
the delicate leaves

swaying in the light wind that
touches his own face.

Life moves just beyond the limit
of our powers

having shown us in the moonlight
her whole body.

I remember
needing nothing

but what I could smell and touch
and hear in the minute

eternity between sounds or the long
shimmer of the barley's

green–gold dance on the wind.
My life a spreading ring

of quiet, like the trout's brief
in–breath

at the surface of a river,
like the slow

outward movement of a raindrop
spreading on a still lake.

Like the silence in which I opened my eyes
to that shadow

behind the branch, to see his half-turned
face for a moment

and heard the church bell above the graves
tolling metallically

three times through white mist,
the first

announcing my arrival in the world
the second,

my childhood gone, while the third
held on through mist

as if mourning and anticipating
in one sound and one sight

a young man's new,
and terrible maturity.

MIDSUMMER PRAYER

In midsummer, under the luminous
sky of everlasting light,

the laced structures of thought
fall away

like the filigrees of the white
diaphanous

dandelion turned pure white and
ghostly,

hovering at the edge of its own
insubstantial

discovery in flight. I'll do the same,
watch

the shimmering dispersal of tented
seeds

lodge in the tangled landscape
without

the least discrimination. So let my own
hopes

escape the burning wreck of ambition,
parachute

through the hushed air, let them spread
elsewhere,

into the tangled part of life that refuses
to be set straight.

Herod searched for days looking for
the children.

The mind's hunger for fame will hunt down
all innocence.

Let them find safety in the growing wild.
I'll not touch them there.

THE HALF TURN OF YOUR FACE

The half turn of your face
toward truth
is the one movement
you will not make.

After all,
having seen it
before,

you wouldn't
want
to take that
path again,

and have to greet
yourself
as you are
and tell yourself
what it was like
to have come so far
and all in vain.

But most of all
to remember
how it felt again
to see
reflected
in your own mirror,
the lines
of abandonment
and loss.

And have those words spoken
inviting you back,
the ones you used to say,
the ones you loved
when your body was young
and you trusted
everything you wanted.

Hard to look,
but you know it has to happen
and
that it takes
only the half turn of your face
to scare yourself
to the core.
Seeing again
that strange resolve in your new reflection.

SOMETIMES

Sometimes
if you move carefully
through the forest,

breathing
like the ones
in the old stories,

who could cross
a shimmering bed of leaves
without a sound,

you come
to a place
whose only task

is to trouble you
with tiny
but frightening requests,

conceived out of nowhere
but in this place
beginning to lead everywhere.

Requests to stop what
you are doing right now,
and

to stop what you
are becoming
while you do it,

questions
that can make
or unmake
a life,

questions
that have patiently
waited for you,

questions
that have no right
to go away.

WHEN THE WIND FLOWS

When the wind flows
and the leaves fall
and your own death
comes to greet you
with its slack mouth,

you'll have to ask
forgiveness then
to gain an easy conscience
for the road ahead,
otherwise,
no one will want you
where he comes from.

No, it's not that they're choosy,
it's just that you wouldn't be happy
without his earnest advice
on the learned and
slightly desperate disciplines
of letting go,
no, you wouldn't
get anywhere near the place
without realising
what you'd been missing all along.

He knows you well enough,
he knows you want
the burden to be yours
and yours alone,
and he knows you'd prefer
a hundred hells than a heaven
where you can't cover with a smile
what until now you've hidden
and never spoken in the clear air.

That's why you'll be terrified
when he first arrives and hell
you realize, resembles more
an average life,
half hidden,
never fully spoken,
something you can grow used to.

THE THICKET

The tangle of it all, the briar curve perspective,
the entrance to places you could not go
without being tugged at the edges, caught
by tiny infractions of wool on the sweater,
brought to a twisted halt to unhook.

I would go anyway in old clothes,
free and happy through a necessary wounding,
my knees damp with the earth, the taste of blood
in my mouth like a richer earth.

In the thicket I could be free and observant,
surveying the tiny stages and the curtained dramas,
every further stage of vision leading me back
to smaller and smaller worlds, like a child's
telescoping theater guiding the eye to a tiny backdrop.
In one, I still see the wren, pivoting straight up
on a branch end, in another, the sloes burn on,
calm and content in their soft black light.
I was never afraid in the thicket, never cramped
or contained and even the constrained scurry
of something close but invisible in the brush brought
home to me all the rewards of a sheltered, secret life.
No one knew me in my child's aloneness
by any other names but the ones that called me back
to the quiet den I made in the hedge
and it seemed with this rich, impassable, interiority,
all outer revelation was possible. From those shadows
I looked happily over great green spaces where
an open visibility would render me unseen.

All that summer I thought I could make it last,
never leave the branching world where, permanent
in my innocence, I could sit, a child abroad beyond
the house and call of waving neighbours,
a crouched pilgrim, an apprentice to stealth and silence,
still and sovereign at the center of my shadowed world,
a kind of enclosed womb-like eternity that could
end only with the annunciation that another wider
and wiser eternity was about to begin.

All of that summer as I changed unknowingly
from young boy to young man, as I went in secret
from undifferentiated shadow to clear edged caster
of a shadow, I looked and looked and changed
unknowingly by looking, afraid as it all began
of the strange impatience growing behind my eyes,
the wound of desire opening slowly at the center
of my sight, not knowing at first that that looking
was a new kind of looking, that that dry mouth
of anticipation was prelude to a different form
of speech, that that minute searching of the
stained glass light searching between the branches
was the knowledge of some immanence
I could not imagine, come to find me
until I half felt, half met, the guiding signal
telling me to leave.

Something fought and sought and found me
in the hedge, gripped me with a new intelligence,
arrested me and set me to motion,
brought clarity to silence, set me to grow
and take this body out of hiding,
made me see the shadows stir with new
and revelatory intolerance, the hooked briars
raw with dispensation and beckoning.

An opening in my world come to find me,
bring me out. Some guiding hand lifted
and shone on me, found me in outline,
illumined the way I shaped in the light,
passed on – the red haw of a new season,
swung like a lantern through the sheltering dark.

SLIGO GLEN:
WALKING OUT OF SILENCE

And then, after,
when you'd turned back
by the way you came,
back toward
the mouth of the Glen
you'd entered
noisily just an hour before,
calling to the others
and you reached again,
but this time alone
the invisible line
where
you could mark exactly
when you began to hear
the sounds of the road
and the machines and the blank
cries of everyday commerce,
so that for a moment you could
retrace that one single step
back into the Glen
and immerse yourself
instantly
in the quiet
source of revelation
you had felt
only a moment before,

as if under water,
as if slipping back
into the river
of silence running between
the tree lined walls
and then you could practice
leaving and
returning in your own body,
through your own breath,
inward and outward,
descending and
entering and reentering the silence
and shelter of your own
narrow valley of aloneness,
from interiority
to conversation
and back.

So that you suddenly realized
you were given
the complete and utter gift
of your own transparency,

the revelation of your
own exact boundary with
the world.

The frontier
between silence and speech
exactly
the line you must cross
to give yourself
while saving yourself,

the gleam in your heart
and your eye,
another sun rising,
the old memories alive
after a long night of absence
and the world again
suddenly worth
risking,
worth seeing,
worth innocence,
worth everything.

THE BELL RINGER

Consider the bell
ringer as an image
of the human soul,
he stands foursquare
on the stone flagged
ground, and surrounded
by a circle of communal
concentration
searches in his fixed
aloneness
for a world
beyond straight,
human,
eye to eye
discourse,
in this case
above him,
the collision of metal
worlds chiming
to each bend and lift
of the knees,
letting his weight
bear down
on the rope,
creating out of the heave
and upward pull,
a hollowed out
brass utterance,
a resonant
on-going argument
for his continued presence,
independent

of daily mood
or the necessities
for a verbal
proclamation.

Consider the reason
for his continued
attendance
to the art.
Caught in a committed
circle of constant practice
yet freed in the vertical
from a horizontal
ever present
and exhausting
human participation,
the ultimate arbitration
an over arching,
straight-out
relationship
with sound.

Somewhere above
in the vertical
he touches
another firmament,
his face
lined, preoccupied
or even set
against the world,
can still announce joy
in the sweet resonance

of birth,
or drama
in the long,
extended,
over and over
carillions of
marriage.

No matter
the clarity
or cloudiness
of the day,
he can follow
that out-going tide
of sound right
to the very edge
of the circled
horizon
until it ebbs back
around him
into the center
of things,
pooling
to a more
rhythmic toll,
a deeper,
more concentrated
commemoration,
the knelling way
the world sounds
inside

when
we've heard
the ease and release
of a last breath.

Let him stand there
then
for the human soul,
let his weight
come true on the rope,
the way we want to lean
into the center of things,
the way we want to
fall with the gravity
of the situation
and then afterwards
laugh and
defy it
with an upward
ultimately untraceable
flight,
a great ungovernable
ringing
announcement
to the world
that
something, somewhere,
has changed.

Consider
the bellringer
as one of us,
attempting some

unachieved,
magnificent
difference in the world,
far above
and far beyond
the stone-closed
space
we seem
to occupy.

Below
we're all
effort, listening
and willful concentration,
above,
like a moving sea,
another power
shoulders
just for a moment
the whole burden,
lifts us
against our will,
lets us find
in the skyward pull
a needed antidote
to surface noise,
a gravity against gravity,
a sky shot through stone,
a clear note,
another way to hear
amid
the clamor of the heavens.

MORTALITY MY MISTRESS

Waking at Cliveden

Silence,
the quiet of centuries
in the ancient room
and the sense of others
here before us
as if everyone now
is waking to the same morning
all the others discovered,
looking out
as they did to
the geese flying
north
or south,
the Thames below
feeling
its way
to a distant sea.

And their mortality
is like my mortality,
a hidden lover
with whom we have woken,
someone we
refuse
to acknowledge
to those outside,
looking in,
a secret
we keep
from the waking day.

But today
I know
I will announce her
and walk with
her and show affection
in the public room,
and
this declaration
will be a testament
to the hidden but suspected
in others,
an example
and a surety to the unspoken
and above all
a proclamation
to the unfaithful
who carefully bide
their endless time.

My declaration
will be
absolute.

An arrival
in the here
and the now.

Then
there will
be little else to do.
I will have become like
the madman running
to see the moon
in the window,

the hawk
I saw tracing the cliff edge
above the river.

I will be the man
I have pursued all along
and finally caught.

I will be
all my intuitions
and all my desires
and then I will walk
slowly down the steps
as if dressed in white
and wade into
the water for
a second baptism.

I will be like
someone who cannot
hide their love
but
my joy will become ordinary
and everyday
and like a lover
I will find out
exactly what it is like
to be the happiest, the only one
in creation
to really
understand how much,
I'm just
a hair's breadth
from dying.

WAITING TO GO ON

I lay a handful of walnuts
to dry by the fire,
pile six new apples in a bowl
and wiping the cutting boards
to a woody gleam, clear off
the fine needles
and nubby stalks
that fell from mushrooms
I found this morning,
walking the woods.

I drop potatoes into
soft, simmering water then
lower the oven
to a ticking heat
and turning to the
beautiful stark
inviting coldness of the hearth,
set down
in the fireplace torn paper
and pine cones,
kindling and logs
and kneeling,
coax small flames
to life,
sweeping the hearth
of dust
and ash,
and still kneeling
next to the fire

just beginning
to snap,
I listen behind me
to the slow tick
of the oven expanding,
to a different time,
another measure,
its black heated interior
braising lamb I saw raised
in the fields that spread below
my upstairs window.

Beneath that window, resting
on paper
in the shadows of my desk,
in the laptop's subdued
pulsing glow,
half-finished poems
wait at the frontier between
being written and being done.

Beside them
a gleaming violin
sits cradled in its stand,
the music book
opened
to an ancient,
rhythmic, hard to get,
tune.

All this continual practice,
this sharpening
and attentive presence,

all
this daily fetching and gathering
this constant maturing
and getting ready,
all this slowly
being heated through,
brought to a simmer,
being educated, knowledgeable,
learning through experience,
all this work to have
one complete day
lived just as it should be,
and
all this constant testing
by the world
to see if we are done,
ready, cooked through,
ripe enough to fall,
to be lifted, bitten right into
and consumed ourselves

and then, for everyone
all the
hours of daily
practice just learning to hit
the note,
the conversational note,
the musical note
just right,
wanting it live
with all the other notes.

It must be we are waiting
for the perfect moment.
It must be
under all the struggle
we want to go on.

It must be, deep
down,
we are creatures
getting ready
for when we are needed.

It must be that waiting
for the listening ear
or the appreciative word,
for the right
woman or the right man
or the right moment
just to ourselves,

we are getting ready
just to be ready

and nothing else.

Like this moment
just before the guests arrive
working
alone in the kitchen
sensing a deep
down symmetry
in every blessed thing.

The way
that everything
unbeknownst
to us
is preparing to meet us too.

Just on the other
side of the door
someone
is about to
knock
and our life
is just
about to change

and finally
after all these
years rehearsing,
behind
the curtain,

we might
just be
ready
to go on.

ARRIVALS

Imagine the confines of a long grey corridor
just before immigration at Washington Dulles
airport. Imagine two Ethiopian women amid
a sea of familiar international plastic blandness,
entering America for the first time. Think of
their undulating multi-colored turbans raised
atop graceful heads, transforming us,
a grey line of travelers behind them, into followers
and mendicants, mere drab, impatient, moneyed
and perplexed attendants to their bright,
excited, chattering arrival.

Imagine a sharp plexi-glass turn left and suddenly
before them, in biblical astonishment, like a vertical
Red Sea churning, like the waters barring Moses from
The Promised Land, like Jacob standing before his ladder,
a moving escalator, a mode of rising, a form of ascension,
a way to go *up* they'd never seen before, its steel grey
movement, an interlocking on and up invitation
that brought them and everyone behind them,
to a bemused, complete, and utter standstill.

So that you saw it for the first time as they saw it
and for what it was, a grated river of lifting steel,
an involuntary, moving ascension into who knows what.
An incredible surprise. And you knew, even through
your tiredness, why it made them raise their hands
to their mouths, why it made them give low breathy
screams of surprise and delighted terror. You saw it
as they saw it, a staircase of invisible interlocking
beckoning hands asking them to rise up

independent of their history, their legs or their wills.
And we stopped as we knew we had to now
and watched the first delighted be-turbaned
woman put a sandaled foot on the flat grey
plain at the foot of the moving stair and
straightway withdraw it with a strangled scream,
leaving her sandal to ascend strangely without her
into heaven, into America, into her new life.

Then, holding her friend away, who tried to grab
her, to save her, to hold her back, who pointed
and shouted, telling her not to risk herself,
not to be foolish, she silently watched her shoe,
that willful child, running ahead, its sole intent
to enter the country oblivious to visas and immigration,
above the need for a job, uncaring of healthcare,
pointing toward some horizon she had never dreamt,
intent on leaving only its winged footprint
for her to follow, like a comet's tail, like an omen
of necessity, like a signaled courage, like an uncaring
invitation, to make her entrance with soul and style.

Because she looked up at this orphaned, onward
messenger with her eyes a-blaze, threw off the panicked
clamoring arms of her friend, raised her chin
in noble profile, and with all that other hurrying
clamor of the world behind her, with a busy,
unknowing, corporate crowd at her back and questions
beginning to be asked out loud, she lifted her arms,
clapped her hands, threw back her head and with
a queenly unbidden grace, strode on to the ascending
heaven bound steel like a newly struck film star,
singing the old, high pitched song her children
would hear when she told the story again.

And as her friend below sang,
applauded, danced on the spot
and ululated her companion's arrival,
we stood there behind her,
transfixed, travel weary,
and crammed into the corridor
like extras from some
miraculous scene in the Bible.

While
she ascended,
her arms straight out,
wide eyed and singing.
Into America.

THE HAZEL WOOD

Sometimes it is like this, a crowded
fire-lit kitchen and a face warmed
by the teacup's steaming rim,
the world an utter comfort and a balm,
listening to the hub-hub
and the easy talk, the window etched
with soft rain and the white reflected ellipse
of porcelain caught deep in the tea.

Other times, up in the hazel
wooded shadow beneath the cliff,
crouched in the no-shelter
of the spindled scrub
with hail cracking the limestone
around me and drumming the bluebells flat,
my head bent in the lightning glare
and the hair on my neck
standing straight up in the electric air,
it's more like some edge we're on, everything
sustained by an invisible thread
that's just about to break, the storm a possible
death about to choose or not to choose
one life among all other lives it sees below
and takes us or leaves us, according to the place
we sit or stand, sheltered or not sheltered,
a person struck and gone
or left alone, like this, to live again.

Crouched beneath that cloud
blown sky, under the roar of wind
and the close repeated drum of thunder
through simultaneous light,
I heard a cry
and then through the tumult,
another cry,
looked up into
the bright white under feathers
of two Peregrine Falcons
come straight from the nesting cliff
claws extended,
banking and screaming to see me off,
away from their young, as if to say,
there's danger enough in the world
without you here too, their wild cries
set to the storm in some parallel agitation.

And me below hugging my knees,
wondering whether to stay or go.
The stone fort beneath the wood
struck again and again, each root of light
seeking a swollen sky, as if breaking
into heaven, and loosing on my bare arms
and bent neck, a stinging hail.

Then, in the light, some intensity reached,
some moment beyond individual power,
some decision reached and then redeemed
by the rush of wind in the valley below,
carrying off the shadow and the storm,
but also, the imminence of that other world,
gone now, not here, now, taken, but

to be remembered, after, down in the
kitchen by the fire, sent back down
to my prison of comfort having glimpsed
in the wild, some open door, something
possible, and me alone in the crowd,
clothes steaming in the welcome heat,
escaped back in, shriven,
soaked to the bone,
drinking tea, alive still,
deserving, perhaps, another life.

WHO MADE THE STARS?

Who made the stars?
You asked yourself,
hiding from your friends
while they beat the field with sticks,
shouting you were nowhere,
had gone to earth,
were drowned
or gone back home,
half-hiding from them
half-hearing them
as they walked away,
their mutual horror
tinged with story-telling awe,
-how they'd tell
they'd lost you,
their lark-flighted calls
dropping from that darkening sky,
remembering as they did,
with dread delight,
the image of your waiting mother.

They left the field shouting
straight into that oblique
horizon of darkness
where you hid, and still
the short and shadowed
length of your hardly breathing
body laid between the moorland
hummocks could not be seen.

Ten years old, alone in the night,
and you, a shadowed Gulliver
in a forest of sedge
grown small beneath those skies,
making yourself
in that covert, rustling
moorland nest,
a tiny nothing
beneath a great question.

Who made the stars?
You said and gave yourself
in that black answering nothing,
to nothing you could speak,
–to their scattered oblivion,
–to their tiny, lit,
concentrated silences,
–to their pin-prick calling
incandescence, and then,
like a quiet revelation,
stealing into you
–to those tiny whispers
ghosting imperceptibly
from nowhere,
–to a child's thought
of God above you
lighting the stars
one by one, or singing them
to light, or casting them
like seed from a white hand,
you were abducted by
that question,
held against your will,

stolen by the river current
of darkness, the images
eddying and turning
above the moor,
the broad black sky
taking you up
from friends and family,
bearing you on
in the night as if floating
toward the bathing milky
roof of stars.

You held on though,
tight to that question
like a raft in the dark,
refusing the rising waters
until you knew
what called you back,
what infinitesimal
pre-word world
had made a hundred
thousand other worlds
to talk to you
and draw you out.

I remember that vast
unspoken talk that night
and your eye
following Orion,
his bent bow
firing into nothing.
I remember
you plumbed the night,

looking along
that lost trajectory,
looking and also
listening
for the first promise
that had promised you,
the first imperceptible
vow that set
all other vows in train,
the original pledge
that made you,
such a small unknown,
able to think upon
a great unknown
and you asked
and asked again
as if to steady against
the current.
Who made the stars?

On the ground
your mind became
a wide scythe
in the field that night,
young and reaching,
supple and tireless,
determined amid the drama
to reap the full arc
of that glimpsed infinity,
you knew some hand
had made the stars
a harvest for your eyes

but what unknown and
ranging pulse
had filled the hand
itself with life?
And then what great
and universal blood
had made the pulse?
And what, what first
embryonic,
and finite
pre-dark beat
had stirred a heart
that brought it all to life?

There in the darkness
and the low trough
of the peat stained ground,
your head beginning to ache
to the beat of origin
after origin,
going back
before the first strike
of anything against
anything,
before the first light
or even
the absence of anything
to perceive the light
and the lost unspoken past
from which it grew,
you felt your own pulse
quicken in the search
and your body

forming round the loose
question,
suddenly draw tight.

Something was near you now,
shaping at the moor's horizon,
your head filling
with questions and origins
until gravity and your small body
were one long road together,
which you, beyond all reach
of common fascination,
traveled as if dreaming,
into the night sky,
caught by the face
of some great presence
looking to you and listening
for the answer.

I remember you disappearing
down that road, moving
quickly toward those eyes.
I know now, looking back,
your body shivered
in the dark,
on the broad moor,
but you were not afraid.

No. Who made the stars?
You said again. Everything
depended on that knowing,
your head still aching,
your mind and heart

so given to everything then,
without articulation,
but sensing that by answering,
speaking and listening
could become
one holy continuity
of experience for which you would
leave all origins to know.

No answer then
but the ache
of that wanting,
no answer then
but the innocence
of a growing
need to know,
enlarging and
expanding
as the world expands
and we beneath it,
our face breathed upon
by angels, trying to grow
beyond the mind
that names a star
to make it void,
to stop the question's
pure gravity
working on the asker.

The child does ask
with a fledgling mind,
reaches the very edge
of the nest

then impotently turns away,
goes home to the lighted house
forgetting and remembering
as he should,
flies off again
as the years pass,
from every edge
in the world but the one
he stood upon that night,
afraid of the vastness
of the flight,
the unknown and unspoken
invitation
to a certain disappearance
and caught
in the growing business
of making all
dark and hidden
promises real
in the lighted world,
he hopes still
amongst it all
to return,
back to the question's
original, stark
and raw ability
to ask and ask
and ask again,
until the question's pure
confrontation
can bring him home,
until like this
the man

the child became
walks back
to lie beneath the stars,
ready
to ask again
to go out for the great meeting,
to vanish from sight,
just as he did, the missing,
innocent child,
but now without
the notion of escape,
no mother or father
to call you back,
no life to live as a consequence
of all this wonder but
a homecoming back to wonder,
a settling deeply
into awe and surrender,
like a gifted premonition
of a good death,
a breathing easy
at the last
and a deep draw
to the memory now
as if going forward,
back to that early evening light
and the stars just beginning
to appear again,
your friends beating the ground
to find you, and you nowhere,
gone to earth
beneath the grass line,
into the question.

[IV]
THE WELL

INSIDE

Inside this sitting here: –
this mind pulling knees up
           close to the chest
           with tense hands.

Inside this
movement of anxiety for the body
and its worries of money
and its teeth grinning falsely
to the solution of all things surrounding

is the seed
and the hands pressing down into the soil
and the dreams of generation
in the seed about to wake.

Tonight I will sleep with my worries
through dreams dark with soil
and the heaving cataclysm of the spade
turning earth round me
not speaking of air
or light fused with greenness
but of darkness
and the first leaves
like hands in prayer
clasped inside the seed.

FAITH

I want to write about faith,
    about the way the moon rises
       over cold snow, night after night,

faithful even as it fades from fullness,
    slowly becoming that last curving and impossible
    sliver of light before the final darkness.

But I have no faith myself,
    I refuse it the smallest entry.

Let this then, my small poem,
    like a new moon, slender and barely open,
    be the first prayer that opens me to faith.

THE WELL OF GRIEF

Those who will not slip beneath
    the still surface on the well of grief,

turning down through its black water
    to the place we cannot breathe,

will never know the source from which we drink,
    the secret water, cold and clear,

nor find in the darkness glimmering,
    the small round coins,
        thrown by those who wished for something else.

FORGIVE

I arrived at last, five hours before she died,
through airport and grounding fog at Heathrow
and the crowded irrelevance of King's Cross.
On the train north toward her I read the paper
with a close, obsessive, intelligence,
knowing I couldn't face the relevance of the day.
Amid a crowd, we live a strange anonymous maturity,
not knowing how deep inside the body,
or how, with each turned leaf of experience
the word *mother* lies waiting to be read again.
In the paper there was no news of her going,
no witness to the courageous continuation
beneath the mask to breathe until I got there.
I travelled as freely in my health as she
struggled mightily to wait, as if we held together,
so far apart, and each in our struggle
opposing corners of creation.
She would let go of her corner
of our world only when she saw me again
for a last time. Imagine then,
the necessity for rest
before the great sweep
of her unspoken life into mine.

THRESHOLD

There were words in the end,
and an unlooked for passionate goodbye,
a song for my father in the few moments
she was allowed to take off the mask,
and my own name said once with the
incredible effort of the last. Then we were all
words, helpless silence, or involuntary
movement in the room, myself telling
her she could go or stay,
my sister saying she was going to meet
the mother she hadn't seen since
she was thirteen, almost shouting
she's waiting for you, the numbers
on the machine steadily dropping
and my father's restless hands unable
to brace the fall. My other sister
ignoring the machine, looked
straight into my mother's eyes,
fierce and unrelenting,
proud of her right and refusal to relinquish
and my mother's eyes equal to hers,
looked back in a fierce companionship
from far inside her going.

Then I heard my own voice again,
as if discovering some marvel
in her face, the knife-edge of a consummate
unlooked for joy, as she turned to go
where we could not follow.
My voice broke from some high
window that was not in the room
and I said look, *look, she's going,*
in unwanted happy astonishment
surprised at the reversal
said as it was, like a young boy
all love and innocent broken promises
anticipating her arrival,
running to a door to greet her again.

FISHING

After her death, I sat by the river
in Burnsall under the sign of the Red Lion,
where we used to sit companionable
looking out over drinks and the mellow stone
bridge to the stream beyond,
taking our casual proximity for granted,
shifting easily in our measured
taken-for-granted sovereign rights,
as two people together, still alive,
moving from talk, to silence, to joke.

And I thought of her now
in some bright nowhere
and me left casting into places
I'd never reached before, the line curling
against a sky she could not see,
fishing in the heady flow
for a dart or a glimmer,
just a remembrance
in the moving mirror
and sensing for the first time
the grip of a pure
and flowing absence.

So strange it was
to slip away
in the stream
from a hard won
maturity,
to feel abandoned,
the line spooling,
the bridge gone,
even the ground aswim,
a river going nowhere,
my hook snagging on thin air
and nothing hidden
in the flowing world
to catch, or bite, or tug again.

THE SHELL

An open sandy shell
on the beach
empty but beautiful
like a memory
of a protected previous self.

The most difficult griefs,
ones in which
we slowly open
to a larger sea, a grander
sweep that washes
all our elements apart.

So strange the way
we are larger
in grief
than we imagined
we deserved or could claim
and when loss floods
into us
like the long darkness it is
and the old nurtured hope
is drowned again,
even stranger then
at the edge of the sea,
to feel the hand of the wind
laid on our shoulder,
reminding us
how death grants
a fierce and fallen freedom

away from the prison
of a constant
and continued presence,
how in the end
those who have left us
might no longer need us,
with all our tears
and our much needed
measures of loss
and that their own death
is as personal
and private
as that life of theirs
which you never really knew,
and another disturbing thing,
that exultation
is possible
without them.

And they for themselves
in fact
are glad to have let go
of all the stasis
and the enclosure
and the need for them to live
like some prisoner
that you only wanted

to remain incurious
and happy in your love,
never looking for the key,
never wanting to
turn the lock and walk
away
like the wind,
unneedful of you,
ungovernable,
unnamable,
free.

FAREWELL LETTER

She wrote me a letter
after her death
and I remember
a kind of happy light
falling on the envelope
as I sat by the rose tree,
on her old bench
at the back door,
so surprised by its arrival,
wondering what she would say,
looking up before I could open it
and laughing to myself
in silent expectation.

Dear son, it is time
for me to leave you.
I am afraid that the words
you are used to hearing
are no longer mine to give,
they are gone and mingled
back in the world
where it is no longer
in my power
to be their first
original author
nor their last
loving bearer.
You can hear
motherly
words of affection now
only from your own mouth

and only
when you speak them
to those
who stand
motherless
before you.

As for me I must forsake
adulthood
and be bound gladly
to a new childhood.
You must understand
this apprenticeship
demands of me
an elemental innocence
from everything
I ever held in my hands.

I know your generous soul
is well able to let me go,
you will in the end
be happy to know
my God was true
and I find myself
after loving you all so long,
in the wide,
infinite mercy
of being mothered myself.

P.S. All your intuitions were true.

LOOKING

My mother is a young girl again
standing at the edge of a field
near The Milepost,
ready to leave.

Across the field
invisibly, we stand together,
together and each alone,
waiting for her to see us,
her son, her daughters,
her husband.

We raise our hands
to catch her sight
but she cannot see us,
she is too young for us yet,
she only sees the sky
and the green fields beneath,
the way young eyes do
and she looks at the road
leading away
toward us
and feels on her skin
the clear breath of sunlight.

She is made for the world
in her own way,
she is life about to make life,
she is a youth about to blossom
out of a particular tragedy
into her own kind of triumph.

She is herself
but
she is all of our past
and all of our future too,
she is looking and waiting
as we wait,
for everything to come true.

DANCE NIGHT
IN WATERFORD CITY

When you had that dream
in your hospital bed,

the first time
we almost lost you,

standing by the door
with your uncle John,

and the whole dance hall
lined with faces

who had known you at sixteen,
it seemed the full tide

of your young life
had swept up to you again

like a long loving circle
of perfect recognition.

How are you then, May,
back to see us all?

And you turned to John
who was laughing

with the rest of them
and asked him what

was behind the door?
And he turned back

and looked at it himself
and said, *May, you don't*

want to go through there
just yet. But in the dream

you knew you wanted
to open the door

and when you found
yourself leaning down

on the handle
as if to go through,

didn't you feel
those two hands

firmly in the middle
of your back

and didn't John
push you from the door

with such a full
determination

that it woke you up,
and there we all were

round your bed
to welcome you back

and that was
the moment

you started to get better,
so that thanks to John

we had three more years
and thanks to the lot of them,

all gathered to meet you,
we know you might have been met now

and be well taken care of
and that somewhere

at the bottom of the dark well
of our going, there's another

door of hospitality,
another recognition,

that the old intuitions
might be true

about being watched over
and that the timing

of it all is not entirely
in our hands but held

in common with every
other hand we've touched

and that the first revelation
after death might be

some kind of gathering,
the first summation something like

a dance night in Waterford City
at the height of our youth,

the tide of faces
ready to meet and welcome us back,

our old body and our young
body, in one body,

greeting and meeting, half aware
and half unaware

of going or returning, the hands pressing
you back to our world

or the door opening this time
to a new light,

an astonishment of welcomes,
a surprise party,

the true dream beneath the first dream.

ANCESTRAL

Far up and off
behind my mother's voice,
my mother's *mother's* voice,
like a lark call
above the dark meadows
of sleep,
a high up
pure and
sudden annunciation,
a strain she'd
carried all along
and me caught
in the song,
slipping
off to other voices,
my father's, father's,
father's work
in the fields
over Hartshead,
my mother's, father's father
fighting
from village to village
and the body
of my father's brother
rolling in the
channel tides.

Each life a traveler
not yet really arrived,
like passing strangers,
the lanterns

half cloaked,
showing a glimmer
at the doors
of the living,
half
looking for
shelter,
half wanting
to stumble on
beyond us
to what waits,
some place perhaps
in the brimming dark
where
the story ends.

STEPPING STONES

I was always half-asleep
and half in love
with that shadowed face
leaning down
and
whispering
the syllables of an intimate
handed down
familial history,
all poverty,
wistfulness
and dreamy cadence,
the light
on the landing
burning behind her
and me beneath
the silhouette listening
to the footfalls
of her past,
how she came to me,
her
life always
seeming to be
approaching
mine, now
and forever.

How she had
lost my brother
and how much
ground we could have
roamed together

her talking
in the half dark
as if he
were here now
with us,
beside the passing stream.

And then the need
some nights
to tell me where she came from
and how I arrived
in the midst
of them all,
the fathers and the brothers
and the one sister,
a story
I would finish
and pass on
as they had,
the stream
of it all,
the passing flow
and me
half swept away
in the story
half gone
elsewhere,
listening
for her,
my head on the banked
pillow
amid
the rippling

and the ebb,
the sleep
of her voice
like soft-shod feet
crossing
on stepping stones,
over the river
and away.

TEMPUS OMNIA REVELAT

The gold hands of the clock
on Hartshead church tower,
reflecting clear winter light
through the windscreen
as I drive back home with the tea
and the bread and the milk
and the thought of my father's
difficult breathing coming to an end
after the nursing and worrying
and midnight conversations
and the closeness of it all this
last three years and my two
sisters by him in my mind
in the room by the window
where this western
light floods them all
and the sudden thought
he might go without me
after all the panicked flights
and a.m. arrivals, the conspiratorial
whispered welcomes at the door
and the sitting by him again
as he rallied and laughed
at the glimpse of my face
come out of nowhere, out of his
jumbled wonderful memory,
all thrown together like a blessed
mercy, so that he could see me
as a man and a boy in the same
sight and reach out his hand

and see my mother there
and not there, according to the
fancy of the light, and be happy
in the arms of my sisters as if
time meant nothing now but its final
heft and weight in the balance
of everything he'd done and
traveled and become.

I turned the corner then,
by the Grey Ox Inn
and looked directly at the lit
church tower,
not *at* the time, but it seemed
at time itself
and knew exactly
when I would arrive,
and when he would go
and then how the light would be
and how the three of us
would come in close
to say goodbye,
the gold light of his going
blessed, unbidden,
by that invisible, omniscient,
careful, Midas touch.

[V]
WRITING

SEVEN STEPS FOR COMING HOME

Oh pure contradiction . . . Rilke

One step to take notice
the next one to look and to praise
the third *to be* praised
the fourth is strangely for love
the fifth is to be
caught between water and sky.

The sixth is return
the seventh unspeakable
except in
one small stolen poem
flawed by the heart
spoken to one another
in secret
never to be said again.

After this look down at the paper
and see who is writing.
Your hands! Only your hands!

A pure contradiction,
a pure blessing.
Everything you learned
has come to nothing.

MUSE

The words insistent, wishing to be said,
   I walk back to the house, find the room lit,
a woman illuminated, by a table with flowers,
   needle in hand, her long fingers threading the cloth
with dark red thread. She turns to look.

The house is quiet, the wind shivers behind me,
   there is a single drop of blood on her hand.

THE TASK AT HAND

As I sit here writing,
the boys outside are stacking wood.

There is the sound of split rounds
thrown into an empty barrow,

dropped on bricks, thrown against the wall,
dropped on the floor and thrown again.

There is the heavy thud of stacking,
the light click of arranging,

a symphonic cacophony of chit-chat,
shouted advice, the radio

blasting at a low volume they are sure
I cannot hear.

There are raised voices, subtle arguments,
and laughing, a marvellous

robust and entirely appropriate
four-letter word as the wheelbarrow falls

over and over, down the steps, onto the terrace,
spilling logs, cartwheeling to oblivion.

Faced with this, the page should remain blank
and by God, after much effort, it does.

ONE DAY

One day I will
say
the gift I once had has been taken.

The place I have made for myself
belongs to another.
The words I have sung
are being sung by the ones
I would want.

Then I will be ready
for that voice
and the still silence in which it arrives.

And if my faith is good
then we'll meet again
on the road
and we'll be thirsty,
and stop
and laugh
and drink together again

from the deep well of things as they are.

THE PAINTER'S HAND

You start
with a painter's hand
working up color
from a dark palette
of remembrance.

It used to be guess-work
touching the pigments
as if they might at any point
betray the startling vision
of its need to live.

Now the paint itself startles
and the hand darting
to the blank canvas
returns the color whole
to the remembered world
from which it came.

Wrong touches
make the blood freeze
a moment before contact.

A color's deepening field
of visual gravity's
deflected a moment before
it pulls the image down.

The fierce eye
of remembrance
finding the eye
of eternal presence
absolves
the mind
of its struggle to live.

The blaze of yellow
Vincent
mistook for God
reveals again
its sacred name.

The light from the window
traveling home
becomes
in the flattened brush
a journey
complete.

Now something
outside the window
high in the branches
of the fiery trees
announces that other
hidden and unseeable
name of light
falling onto
the stretched canvas
where my hand moves
firmly.

The artist gladly resigns
his freedom
in the split second
when the hand feels the brush
halt on the painting's
opening world.

The lost world
where we live
and remember
not wishing freedom
for a moment.

THE POET

moves forward
to that edge
but lives sensibly,

through the senses
not because of them.

Above all he watches
where he steps.
As if it matters
where he leaves his prints.

The senses overwhelm him
at his peril.

Though he *must* be taken
by something greater.
That is what he uses
senses to perceive.

The poet's

task is simple.
He looks for quiet,
and speaks to what
he finds there.

But like Blake
in his engraving shop, works
with the fierceness
of acid on metal.

Melting apparent
surfaces away
and displaying
the infinite
which was hid.

In the early morning
he listens
by the window,
makes
the first utterance
and tries to overhear
himself
say something,
from which
in that silence,
it is impossible to retreat.

THE BODY IN FULL PRESENCE

The body in full presence
holds its first creative essence
in the pen that touches paper.
Lifting the glass that holds the wine,
this beckoning uncertainty is mine.

I'll follow my line to an early death,
feeling out rhythm in the spoken breath
and startled by flame
this arrogance shall be my moth,
flying with his burning cloth.

Then humility will rise
out of poetry's deep surmise,
and I will have confidence in my powers;
wanting this presence, burnt by the past,
I'll die in the first line – and become the last.

NO ONE TOLD ME

No one told me
it would lead to this.
No one said
there would be secrets
I would not want to know.

No one told me about seeing,
seeing brought me
loss and a darkness I could not hold.

No one told me about writing
or speaking.
Speaking and writing poetry
I unsheathed the sharp edge
of experience that led me here.

No one told me
it could not be put away.
I was told once, only,
in a whisper,
"The blade is so sharp-
It cuts things together
-not apart."

This is no comfort.
My future is full of blood,
from being blindfold,
hands outstretched,
feeling a way along its firm edge.

FOUR HORSES

On Thursday the farmer
put four horses
into the cut hay-field
next to the house.

Since then the days
have been filled with the
sheen of their
brown hides
racing the fence edge.

Since then I see
their curved necks
through the kitchen window,
sailing like swans
past the pale field.

Each morning
their hooves fill my
open door
with an urgency
for something
just beyond my grasp

and I spend my whole
day in an idiot joy,
writing, gardening,
and looking
for it
under every stone.

I find myself
wanting to do
something
stupid and lovely.

I find myself
wanting to walk up
and thank
the farmer for those
dark brown horses and
see him stand
back laughing in his
grizzled and
denim wonder at my
innocence.

I find myself wanting
to run down First Street
like an eight year old,
saying, "Hey!
Come and look
at the new horses
in Fossek's field!"

And I find myself
wanting to ride
into the last hours
of this summer,
bareback and
happy as the hooves
of the days
that drum toward me.

I hear the whinny of
their fenced and abandoned
freedom
and feel happy
today
in the field
of my own making,

writing non-stop,
my head held high,
ranging the boundaries
of a birthright
exuberance.

THIS POEM BELONGS TO YOU

This poem
  belongs to you
    and is already finished,

it was begun years ago
    and I put it away

knowing it would come
  into the world
    in its own time.

In fact
  you have already read it,
    and closing the pages
      of the book,

you are now
  abandoning the projects
  of the day and putting on
    your shoes and coat
      to take a walk.

It has been long years
  since you felt like this.

You have remembered
  what I remembered,
    when I first began to write.

THE LIGHTEST TOUCH

Good poetry begins with
the lightest touch,
a breeze arriving from nowhere,
a whispered healing arrival,
a word in your ear,
a settling into things,
then, like a hand in the dark,
it arrests the whole body,
steeling you for revelation.

In the silence that follows
a great line,
you can feel Lazarus,
deep inside
even the laziest, most deathly afraid
part of you,
lift up his hands and walk toward the light.

MY POETRY

My poetry is all
reversed arrivals,
departures that are not,
secret losses
become public gains
and love welling
from the wound
of a misconstrued defeat.

In my lines surprises
are no surprises
except
the surprise of forgetting
how close we are
to a total disappearance.

That's why I have to say it
and repeat it.
That's why I need to
write it down,
that's why I have
to look in the mirror
and then
sometime after
shout it
from the rooftops
of a blank page.

That's why I have
to surprise myself
and disturb everyone else,
even tell strangers
and people not yet
born or imagined,
that's why
without poetry
it's so easy to lie
day after day
about unbelievable
and unspoken truths,
that's
why it's
so easy to
tell and retell
without knowing,
without shame,
the same
old broken stories,
again
and again
and again.

MARINER

Surrounded by stones and trees
and circling the village on foot,
we saw the tense wind begin to swirl
red leaves among the roots
and tasted at last in our mouths,
the first dry culminating dust
of a summer's end.

I realized then,
the sudden annunciation,
the quick beginning all at once
of something that had
until now, only a slow
interior formation,
and I turned my face naturally
into the eye of that wind,
like the keel of some intuitive vessel
rearing toward the
source of the blow,
from that direction
I felt impending danger
and freedom and even across that
interior landscape,
the whole sway
and fetch of a sea.

Above me, peacocks
screamed on a high wall,
stretching their necks
to the bronze-shot clouds,
the chestnut trees
shook their leaves in a mass,
then above them,
a skyward rustle of doves
like upswung leaves,
a quick, tightening of the throat
and the full storm broke upon us
like a wave.

The whole world
was movement then
even before the first
premonitory clap
of thunder rolled across the Downland,
and I, young again in the involuntary
necessities of a rough creation,
ran off and left the path,
found shelter from the sudden searing light
in the door of a barn piled with bales
and the pungent yeast of decaying straw.

Separated from friends and glad to be alone,
forty six and looking for some secret
memory I'd hidden from myself,
the air freshening even as it frightened,
the heart alive and broken open
to its own sudden, unloved
and necessary demise.

The robust inclinations of a spirit
long covered by necessity began
to touch a future still waiting
to be met. In the reek
of hay and the upward whirl of dust,
I felt youth again, not as memory
now but a forceful anticipation,
something yet to come.
As if the hand of someone
once alive in the memory
had reached through confusion
and touched me again.
The horizon all implication
and extended invitation
to sudden arrival.
All the elemental forces
of the world a pure revelation.
This day my life,
this body a ground
on which to stand,
this weather a sea,
and my sense of self
a strange shoreline
on which it broke and fell.

My hand lifted to parse the light.
I remembered kneeling as a child
over the new worlds I'd seen charted
on a blank and open page,
me there on the kitchen floor,
a small, devoted figure,
reading Coleridge over and over,
my bent head
compelled to the fearful journey
like an intuited prayer for my whole life,
some child in me
abroad in the storm
inclined once more
to the old wonder
and my heart moved to write it all again.

[VI]

REMEMBER

WHERE MANY RIVERS MEET

All the water below me came from above.
All the clouds living in the mountains
gave it to the rivers,
who gave it to the sea, which was their dying.

And so I float on cloud become water,
central sea surrounded by white mountains,
the water salt, once fresh,
cloud fall and stream rush, tree roots and tide bank,
leading to the rivers' mouths
and the mouths of the rivers sing into the sea,
the stories buried in the mountains
give out into the sea
and the sea remembers
and sings back,
from the depths,
where nothing is forgotten.

SONG FOR THE SALMON

For too many days now I have not written of the sea,
nor the rivers, nor the shifting currents
we find between the islands.

For too many nights now I have not imagined the salmon
threading the dark streams of reflected stars,
nor have I dreamt of his longing,
nor the lithe swing of his tail toward dawn.

I have not given myself to the depth to which he goes,
to the cargoes of crystal water, cold with salt,
nor the enormous plains of ocean swaying beneath the moon.

I have not felt the lifted arms of the ocean
opening its white hands on the seashore,
nor the salted wind, whole and healthy,
filling the chest with living air.

I have not heard those waves,
fallen out of heaven onto earth,
nor the tumult of sound and the satisfaction
of a thousand miles of ocean,
giving up its strength on the sand.

★

But now I have spoken of that great sea,
the ocean of longing shifts through me,
the blessed inner star of navigation
moves in the dark sky above
and I am ready like the young salmon,
to leave his river, blessed with hunger,
for a great journey on the drawing tide.

VISION ON THE HILLS

That full view of the world seen as a child,
barely understood, a flight of half-remembered doves
and red leaves in violent rustle from the wind that followed.

Stone walls climbed the hilltops through thunder
and sleeting rain, entering the mist that drew me on
paths where every stone stood single, opening like eyes

to other worlds, the black-faced sheep snaking
out of moss and the stone-barns buttressed by
old stones and an older time to which I knew,

by seeing this, by seeing *now*, belonged to me
as I to them, welded by the heat of full attention
sustained by time, held up for all by youth

too caught in the ordinary
miracle to worry what was past
and what was present, or beyond it,

whether the bright vision itself could fade.
It could, it did. It seems we slide down the long
curve of years falling through time until we wake

or dream like this: the window open
to find us, brazen miracle,
momentary fresh, before we lose our faith again.

Almost desperate, searching through the crowded years,
we meet ourselves a final time, try to touch him,
hold him by the shoulders, teach us how to see again.

Our hands climb bewildered to our eyes,
too late we see everything, we ask everything.
Who lost that vision? Who? Who lost that vision?

TIME LEFT ALONE

The standing stones are silent, the ground will not speak,
the half-moon flares in a dark sky, locking them in shadow.
How many times, blindfold by time, staring out through starlight
or before dawn at the dreamless face of the sea about to wake
have young men entered the waves and left the shore-line forever?

Our fathers no longer speak of this or turn their lined faces
to walls white-washed by moon-light, seeing the same walls
their own fathers saw, hoping the same half-hopes, unable
to let time go, finding only as the needle's dropped in death,
the breath's a thread pulled in and out of the present.

But tired of land, we open ourselves to oceans, tired of time
we give back all that we've taken, tired of ourselves
we open ourselves to ourselves at last, sensing the waves
and great abyss of the sea beyond, the ocean stretching on sand
and the long view on the still sea that leads to another life.

And we go out as the fish go out, leaving the taste
of the rivers we know, joining the dark invisible weight
of what we would become, the calm sense of movement
seeing the others forming our shoals, and the scales
on our sides filling the depth with trembling stars.

In that depth, return's instinctual, the moon harvests
the long years and binds them in sheaves in a circle,
and we return too, for home from the sea we come to the river,
turning the ocean's face toward land, opening to silence
as the salmon opens to the sweet water in a saltless stream.

Then out of the rivers we're taken again, returned to a land
we hardly remember, as out of memory we come to our senses
walking the cold night, this sea of blades stirred slightly
by a shifting breeze, this half-known need to know
what others hardly knew themselves, this silence in the stars

leading to the dawn's first edge of sky and a silence
in ourselves that has no resolution. We would forget
if we could what all this meant, our fathers forgot
how giving up our need for time, we join a greater time,
and so these early years are years for growing old,

older than our fathers could. To let time be alone
outside of what we need. To hold it where it's held in trust,
beyond our need for time itself. Where the hand's grasp
opens in surprise and fear, to find itself full, and the face
that opens at last can see itself new. Full in the depth of the sea.

WHAT IT MEANS TO BE FREE

We sit on the plane, we watch,
we see clouds, grey hills,
the road edged with fuchsia,
and from a vision, near Bantry,
an old man walking on the wet road.

Behind him the light opens
in a long arch across the sea.
He has a stick, a hat, old shoes,
a gait that says he will walk forever.

He reaches out, touching the bright
bell-like overhanging flowers with his stick.
His face lifts, catching the light as I look
out the window through deep veils
of cynicism and irony flooding the landscape.

From his face I look down at my book
into the dark interior of the plane,
surprised by the single tear.
Knowing how long it took – even to feel.
Now it seems after years of walking,
the homecoming happened in a single step.

The imagination cradled so long
returns grown with its manly gift
and the shut bud of my emotion
opens like a flower on the white page.

HORSE IN LANDSCAPE: FRANZ MARC

We know the fiery animality
of the purebred horse,
its ghostly hide moving like smoke
over the green landscape.

But must remember
in that wild vulnerability
a natural power of rest.

Marc did it with a bold gesture.
Painted the neck
rising to the curved horizon
and its blue mane swelling in waves.

Primary colors and prime emotion
swirl in the coiled flank.
Head rearing to the pasture's expanse.

The landscape living in its body
as the sinewy horse lives in the world.

Now, as it turns toward you,
head curved to one side
and the wild mane flying
above the distant hoof beats'
incantatory silence,
you are asked again—

What will you do
and what will you say
in the times
when you are left alone
to meet, like this,
the quiet fury of the world?

YOU DARKNESS

You darkness from which I come,
I love you more than all the fires
that fence out the world,
for the fire makes a circle
for everyone
so that no one sees you anymore.

But darkness holds it all:
the shape and the flame,
the animal and myself,
how it holds them,
all powers, all sight–

and it is possible: its great strength
is breaking into my body.

I have faith in the night.

Rainer Maria Rilke   *Trans. D. W.*

THE WELL OF STARS

Blue lights on the runway like stars
on the surface of a well
into which I fall each night from the sky,
emerging through the tunnel door
of the jetway, and the black waters
of the night, in the cities of America.

In the lit rooms of glass and steel,
in the still and secret towers,
under the true stars hid by cloud
and the steam shrouded roofs
of the mansions of money and hope,
I come with my quiet voice and
my insistence, and my stories,
and out of that second and
deeper well I see again those other
blue stars and that other darkness,
closer even than the night outside,
the one we refuse to mention,
the darkness we know so well
inside everyone.

I have a few griefs and joys
I can call my own
and through accident it seems,
a steadfast faith in each of them
and that's what I will say
matters when the story ends.

But it takes a little while to get there,
all the unburdening
and the laying down
and the willingness
to really tire of yourself,
and then step by step,
the way
the poets through time
generously gave themselves
to us,
walking like pilgrims
through doubt,
combining their fear,
their fierceness and their faith.

And you now,
in the front of the room
under the fluorescent light
by the reflected window,
hiding all the stars
you have forgotten.

One more member
of the prison population
whose eyes have caught
the open gate at last.
You are the one for whom the gift was made.

Keep that look in your eyes
and you'll gladly grow tired of your reflection.

All this way through
the great cloud race between
here and Seattle, just
to look beneath your face.

There, for all to see,
the well of stars,
and the great night from which you were born.

ONCE ROUND THE MOON

Once round the moon,
your mother would say,
sitting you on the draining
board to wipe your face

as your legs swung like clock-
work under the curtain,
her ritual night-words allowing
you to signal a grave nodded

permission for the cleansing act
and your irritation at being washed,
dissolving in the mesmerizing flight
of damp flannel skimming your face,

its orbit incidentally cleaning
and shining as it went.
Once round the moon she'd say
and then she'd do it again, hunting

for the parts she'd missed,
which of course, was twice
round the moon, but you didn't
mind so long as she'd said it again,

her face smiling at the very center
of the circle so you could travel
happily round the circumference
of her fancied world,

your own face glowing
in the moon–cold passage
of the cloth and your mother's
voice a safe companion to the journey,

so that you were both whisked away
and safe as houses, kept to the task
and let go, allowed to wander
in your mind wherever you wanted

but engaged to comply through affection.
Then, after the cloth had gone,
and like another flight, you'd be lifted up
and over, your nose almost touching

hers and passed around the room to say good night.
The way, the rest of your life you'd be carried
from place to place and person to person,
far from the atmosphere of that crowded room.

The way you return again and again, caught
by tides of affection and remembrance,
pulling you back as if you were actually
going forward into a further understanding

of how you were first brought into the world
and then given away to others. *Once round
the moon* she'd say, holding onto you
while setting you on a course far away

into a life you could live as your own,
into a world you thought you had created
entirely by yourself, into the realization
she had travelled most of the way before you.

The way there is a trick to everything,
even to stilling a child with love,
the way all necessary work
has an elemental basis to accomplishment,

even the work of remembering
how everything was, that winter night, so long ago,
the necessary task of remembering and retrieving
the best that I can think of her.

For my mother, always two jobs, two stories,
two worlds even, in one movement,
love and need and nothing
now or ever to separate the two.

LEARNING TO WALK

Walked out this morning
into a broad green garden
with the rising sun in my eyes
and the first hint of the day's heat
touching my face,
feeling as broad as the garden
and young as the day
and soaking up the heat
in my black tee-shirt,
walked straight forward
out of the gate,
through the wood,
along the river,
toward the mountain
and thought of the future
I could make in the world
if I walked toward it
like this,
with my face toward the hills
and my eyes full of light
and the earth sure
and solid beneath me,
walking on
with a fierce anticipation,
and a faithful expectation,
with the sun and the rain
and the wind on my skin
and the old sense
I remember at twenty
of many paths
breaking from one path.

As if the body could walk
forever,
as if we all could walk
and keep on walking
from one path to another,
noting and loving again
the wonders
of the turning world,
calling to each of us like
old friends and new,
discovered and rediscovered,
all of them waiting
like we'd never left them
walking as if we'd always
been faithful,
walking as if sharp and present
enough to know true friends
as we met them,
walking as if
mature enough to keep
them for a lifetime,
walking
as if for instance,
as if for instance,
we all had learned
how
to give all our money away,
watching it return
without a shirt on its back,
happy and singing,
telling stories and introducing
us to brilliant company,
walking as if we could be
dangerous

again,
dangerous
in our generosity,
refusing to save
for our retirement,
upsetting father-in-laws
and financial advisors,
teachers and preachers,
adjudicating journalists,
mothering ministers
and self important judges,
walking as if
enlightened and elegant,
piratical and pragmatic,
abroad in the cross current
conversation of the world,
our solid path
day by day,
becoming beneath our feet,
a sea course,
a heading on a wide horizon,
an ocean's mere inclination to flow,
a compass line to possibility,
a sea edge
of probability.

So learning to walk
in morning light
like this again,
we'll take a first step

toward mortality,
out of the garden,
through the woods,
along the river,
toward the mountain,
its simple,
that's what we'll do,
practicing as we go

and
we'll be glimpsed, traveling
westward, no longer familiar,
a following wave,
greeted, as we were at our birth,
as probable and slightly dangerous strangers,
some wild risk about to break again
on the world.

REMEMBER

So many years since I saw you last,
that I couldn't recognize
your brotherly presence
even as you sat beside me.

So many memories hidden
from a busy present,
that I ate with you without seeing you,
a stranger amongst other strangers,
talking, talking
about nothing in particular.

I wonder, were we ever to meet
with God as we still lived
and breathed, would we do exactly
the same thing,
let time go by
exchanging
pleasantries
about the weather,
not even knowing
how to ask the question?

Once we were one
and now we are two
and the second has grown
and forgotten the first.

The ancient love
we felt a mere fable now,
a story across time,
a distant recognition
across the table,
an ache beneath
the glance and
the seemingly necessary,
ordinary request
to pass the salt.

APOLOGY

Now I know my great success
in the world
was your vulnerability,
my breaking through boundaries
the raw break in your heart
at being left behind.

Now I know
in going forward,
you were waving me on,
in my building sense of presence,
lay the clear choice on your part
to be a foundation.

But now after
all these years,
going forward seems like
coming back to meet you again,
and I want to sit with you
at the midnight table
and reach across
in the silence
and tell you
I shouldn't have gone
and left you the way
I did.

But you'll look at me again
with that old smile
and that sense

in the silence
that you are a *you* that can make
so many *me's* of me.

You have those
eyes after all,
through which I see myself
reflected,
journeying on
through all those beckoning
horizons radiating
from your stillness.

They bring me again
to those frontiers,
those arrivals,
those circles emanating
continually
from the central fact
of your staying.

[VII]
EXILE

WHAT IS IT LIKE?

What is it like to be alone?
To fall into the abyss
where voices do not speak?

What is it like to have
given everything away?
In the *wrong* way?

What is it like to love no one?
To live in a house
shared only by servants?

What is it like?

It is like this.
You are alone beneath a cold moon,
you cannot speak,
the bitter night has pierced your clothes
and when you sleep,
your body stirs with a chill wind
which hour after hour
and against your will,
refuses to stop.

In the cold morning
you will be open
to one comfort only.

The barely conceived surprise
of being shaken awake.

ACTAEON TELLS ALL

I saw a stag through mist, silver,
fleeing from dogs through deep grass and meadow
then back under canopies of cool wood.

Saw her, pale light leaving the water,
lean down, lay her hair over green moss,
while above the legs curving, rising,

I saw a dark place, and the limp arms as if dead
lifted by the ones who bathed her.
Saw her tongue delirious in her open mouth

and small drops of water fall, linger
on the flesh rubbed pink.
Felt myself move unknowing forward,

and sense the strange energy that could
come between us were I to lie on her.
The night inside night and the first dream

at first touch. Snow drifting on white hills
and my warm hands where her secret lies.
Her eyes would leap fire I thought,

but she saw me first, made *me* burn, rear up
from her transformed, brown hooved in sudden leap,
nostrils flared in terror of the distant hounds.

I, now far from her, found a place to rest at last,
because all day between oaks I ran here
with strange horns, gave everything to her,
was bitten, brought down, eaten by my own dogs.

JOHN CLARE'S MADNESS

Northamptonshire's
deadly flat
spreads beneath the hawk.

Watching hedgerows
and the muddy lanes,
sharp eyed for winter he's aware again

how each small movement's plain
to the eye awake
for food or touch of rain

to make his feathers start.
My pen touched paper
just the same. Alert to follow

exactly what I saw. Said
exactly how I speak.
Now,

Northborough's
fields hold nothing,
-my house an empty shell.

Above Helpstone
the hawk circles
the house that I have failed.

There is a small body
caught in his claws,
it cries to the hawk in fear.

I said, beat, beat, strange wings,
what is won then lost
comes back with the fiercest pain.

THIS TIME

This time he has gone
too far.
The chair overturned
on the floor,
the accusation, the door
banging wildly.
He will not return. Everything
he has gained
he is willing to lose.
Is glad to lose.

Because he loved too much
his own redemption.
Because he felt
he could not be touched.
Because he hoped
he would not need that touch.
He is willing to go
where he should not go.

The night is familiar.
The wind is cold.
He has no future,
only the words
"I will not go back."

As the road steepens,
his grief goes ahead,
reaches the top,
turns round, watches him
with the dead child's face.
This is not to be spoken of.

He stopped,
"I will not go back"
trembled through his body.

He did not go back.
He stood, mouth open,
watching the lonely stars
rise from darkness.
He listened. He heard
for the first time
the clear grief of his voice.
He leant against the wall.
He wept. He felt his breath
rising and falling.
Dead already
he had nothing to lose.
He stood up and wavered,
the faint stars glimmering.
A strange dignity
in his bowed head.
A broken man
holding the ashes
of an only child.

He felt himself cradled
by strong arms.
He opened his eyes
in those arms
and saw the stars.

Those stars told him
they loved him only
for what *he* loved himself.
They did not love him
for what he was.

From the dark town
A bell chimed
"Nowhere to go."
A half promise from
the half-killed dream
of his life.
He was the other half.

Something was happening.
Somewhere in the high tower
of the long night
the bell went on chiming.
Destroyed, lost, killed,
but finally, in this new presence
surviving. He would not go back.
He would not go on.

NEVER ENOUGH

It is never enough. The three riders
arrive with gifts. The woman brings food.
The child looks with admiring eyes.

Something else is triggered. He hears
unaccountably the voice of someone he knew.
He pulls back the curtain. No one.
At night he opens his depths
and dreams. He will not appear.
He turns to the old part of himself
known since a boy. Gone.
The door open in the night wind
and on the oak table a note.
"I am to be trusted but you are not."

He remembers everything he can. His face.
His hands. The way he would rise as if to speak.
Oblivion begins to pull on its long shroud.
He has one moment before panic.
His voice ready to pounce on death
unsheathes its secret claws. His hour.
His place. His voice with its new sound.
A bunched animal cornered by stealth.

Then someone gets up, closes the door,
begins to speak.

SECOND BIRTH

The wild dream, two whirling lights
turned one inside the other
and then away. The child's terror
seeing one as his mother,
and that black space opened into nothing,
the hand outstretched
toward the perfect ring
of light becoming other.

And I, after the first birth
and that first unspeaking error,
will undertake a second birth
and so relinquish terror.

NEW YEAR PRAYER

This robust heart involved
with too many worlds
for its own good,
this portion of creation
constantly trying
to make its self singular,
this chef at home in the kitchen
among a gleam of knives,
sommelier
among eclectic bottles,
sometimes dreaming
as a hermit among leaves,
drinking the centuries
of inherited silence,
sometimes the
social host opening
the doors and lighting
the candles,
often a father lifting his daughter
high up above him
and then
the husband
sheltered by night
attempting
to talk and talk again,
too often now
as the years go by
the son worrying
for a father sitting
Atlantic miles away,
in a silent
remembered parallel.

And now this
other parallel,
this symmetry
inside
for everything
on the outside,
the writer in winter
at his desk,
caught in the light,
beneath the window,
bringing together
the last and the first,
the middle and the edge,
the near and the far,
the troubled lives
all calling for the one line
and the one life,
for creation come together
in a central
unspoken wish,
to be held
and made one

like
a god's blessing
out of nowhere,
the pen put down
so the open palm,
warmed and full,
can touch a wound
that heals them all.

[VIII]

THE CONSEQUENCE OF LOVE

PISAC, PERU

I remember those trees along the water,
a silent sky of clouds
in the river beneath their roots.

I remember you walking
and that silence on the bridge
asking us to stop.

I remember it like this
as if it will happen again,

above water, on a bridge
between two banks,
your dark hair and fierce eyes,

your refusal to go on
and your refusal to give up.

I remember it like this,
and then,
as you begin to speak,
my memory sees only the river
and your face
beneath a pale sky,
flowing away, as if forever.

HUARAS

Those mountains out of my past,
Cordillera Blanca,
blue snow and grey peaks
and a cold wind on the frigid lake.

The calmness in your eyes
for once without fear
for what it might mean
to be together,
traveling south through Peru.

I remember you looked up
as if there might be promise
in something I might say or do.

Your face caught in sunlight
before the momentary cloud
darkened you again.

Above us the storm clouds
gathered everything
greedily,
leaving nothing to say.

Only when the clouds rolled
madly on the grey slopes
and we ran in the thunder
did I take your arm,
speaking too quickly
what needed to be said.

Ten years later and I still
don't understand your answer,
and like then, after the storm,
we are still walking together,
two solitaries
moving apart in the falling rain.

AYACUCHO

A cold wind off the mountain
as the grey light lies flat
on the ground where we walk.

Whoever looks back on this time
will only see two people
united in misunderstanding.

I know you will say this
is not so, there were other
darker compunctions
which held us truly
together.

There was the secret
we shared between us
which you would speak
and I would ignore.

There was the line upon line
of blue ridge and ochre mountain,
the dizzy field lines
tipped crazily toward the sky,
the patchworks of tilled earth
and memory
and the bitter Andean earth
turning slowly under
the foot hoe.

In our love of bitterness
we seemed to drink that earth.
Its cold black heart filled
with an old sorrow,
like the young girl in rags
in a sleet-storm of snow
following the sheep
off the hillside.

You asked me not to give
her anything.
I gave it anyway
and you raged
all the way into evening.
It made things worse
you said, as if we could
do something.

Now we look back
there *was* nothing we could do.
She turned into the snow
like someone
moving toward her own ghost.

And now we are all
together again,
you are here,
and she is here,
her cold knuckles
holding her shawl.
She is the one I am glad to see.
And you,
you will not get one word from me.

CUZCO

It became clear
toward evening.
The gold hands
of the high mountains
in a blaze from
the hidden sun,
the streaming light
and the shadows
in the west,
hiding the nested
houses.
The train whistle
streaming
copper-colored smoke
as it left
through the fields
toward Puno.

You would stay
and I would go on.
One story already
becoming old,
how I left you.

Centuries gone by
and the tale will only
get better.
I left by train
to Bolivia,
flew to the north
from La Paz.

Now the fields
are passing
by the window
and the young men
turn toward home,
I remember your face
last night
close to mine,
looking down
on the cobbled streets,
you were a young girl
almost
wanting to begin again.

And I laughed
with you,
a wild faithlessness
to life
gripping me
for a moment.
It could have been
so easy,
one more day,
true to the old promise,
holding the tide of night at bay.

Who wrote this story
that we should meet
and part again?

The indifferent god
we had made ourselves,
faithless as ever to lovers
with plans.

MACCHU PICCHU

This sense of looking down
through green jungle
from the edge of a world
we had chosen together.

As if here, toward evening,
we would know
how to leave,
finally and forever,
all the things
we had *not* chosen.

I remember your hair
and the dark-ridged slopes
of the mountains
flowing together.
The river
thousands of feet
below tumbling
toward dark.

I remember your look
of surprise as you
saw me, a stranger again,
like the first time
looking up from the ocean
you called me by name.

And then, as if
we make meaning
simply in order
to leave it.

We forgot
everything,
looking out
from the mountain
over the walls
of centuries,

the vanishing point
of the sun
extinguishing time
forever,
to the instant
before we had met.

IN A MOMENT OF MADNESS,
A DUBLIN POET THINKS OF
AN OLD LOVE

Twenty years since I knew her.
Wherever she is now, I will go to her.
I know you can never believe me
but her face is as fresh to me
as the winter day we parted.

Once, my life was like a flight
through clear air, searching the field lines
for a high place from which to see.
Now, they have clipped my wings,
turned my proud eagle flight
into the hesitant perching of a shivering wren.

It is in the shape of my old self then,
the hawk, the curlew, or anything wild
that flies against the sky
that I'll find her once again,
staring out from the woods
on a winter evening.

Like this then,
as a soundless shadow of love,
I will fly to the low branch above her.

THE HAWTHORN

The crossed knot
in the hawthorn bark
and the stump
of the sawn off branch,
hemmed by the roughened
trunk. In that
omniscient black eye
of witness,
I see the dark no-growth
of what has passed,
grown round by
what has come to pass,
looking at me
as if I could speak.

So much that was
good in her,
so much in me,
cut off now
from the future
in which we
grew together.

Now,
through the window
of my new house
that hawthorn's
crooked faithful
trunk round
an old and broken
growth,

my mouth dumb

and
Dante's voice,
instead of mine,
from the open book.

Brother, our love
has laid our wills to rest.
Making us long
only for what is ours
and by no other thirst
possessed.

Our life not lived
together,
must still
live on apart,
longing only
for what is ours
alone,
each grow
round the missed branch
as best we can,
claim what is ours
separately,

though not forget
loved memories,
nor that life
still loved by memory,
nor the hurts
through which we
hesitantly
tried to learn
affection.

Our pilgrim journey,
apart or together,
like
the thirst
of everything
to find its true form,
the grain of the wood
round the hatched knot
still
straightening
toward the light.

THE TRUELOVE

There is a faith in loving fiercely
the one who is rightfully yours,
especially if you have
waited years and especially
if part of you never believed
you could deserve this
loved and beckoning hand
held out to you this way.

I am thinking of faith now
and the testaments of loneliness
and what we feel we are
worthy of in this world.

Years ago in the Hebrides,
I remember an old man
who walked every morning
on the grey stones
to the shore of baying seals,

who would press his hat
to his chest in the blustering
salt wind and say his prayer
to the turbulent Jesus
hidden in the water,

and I think of the story
of the storm and everyone
waking and seeing
the distant,
yet familiar figure,
far across the water
calling to them,

and how we are all
waiting for that
abrupt waking,
and that calling,
and that moment
we have to say *yes*,
except, it will
not come so grandly,
so Biblically,
but more subtly
and intimately, in the face
of the one you know
you have to love.

So that when
we finally step out of the boat
toward them, we find
everything holds
us, and everything confirms
our courage, and if you wanted
to drown you could,
but you don't,

because finally
after all this struggle
and all these years,
you don't want to any more,
you've simply had enough
of drowning,
and you want to live and you
want to love and you will
walk across any territory
and any darkness,
however fluid and however
dangerous, to take the
one hand you know
belongs in yours.

LIVING TOGETHER

We are like children in the master's violin shop,
not yet allowed to touch the tiny planes or the rare wood,
but given brooms to sweep the farthest corners
of the room, to gather shavings, mop spilled resins
and watch with apprehension the tender curves
emerging from apprenticed hands. The master
rarely shows himself but whenever he does, demonstrates
a concentrated ease, so different from the wilful accumulation
of experience we have come to expect,
a stripping away, a direct appreciation of all the elements
we are bound, one day, to find beneath our hands.
He stands in our minds so clearly now, his confident back
caught in the light from pale clerestory windows
and we note the way the slight tremor of his palms
disappears the moment they encounter wood.

In this light we hunger for maturity, see it not as stasis
but a form of love. We want the stillness and confidence
of age, the space between self and all the objects of the world
honoured and defined, the possibility that everything
left alone can ripen of its own accord,
all passionate transformations arranged only
through innocent meetings, one to another,
the way we see resin allowed to seep into the wood
in the wood's own secret time. We intuit our natures
becoming resonant with one another according
to the grain of the way we are made. Nothing forced
or wanted until it ripens in our own expectant hands.
But for now, in the busy room, we stand in the child's
first shy witness of one another, and see ourselves again,
gladly and always, falling in love with our future.

MARRIAGE

(Ulysses)

This skin I should shed,
beneath it I am barely visible,
cannot be seen or recognized
or welcomed back,
all you can see are my travels
and they are the least of me,
not the one who has arrived.

I am almost home now.
And you, you are always waiting
beyond that horizon
I must make for myself,
again and again.

You have always waited
and with your clear eyes,
have always known the secret,
how we wait, day by day
for the arrival of an
affection we must first
have made completely our own.

(Penelope)

It has taken ten years
Ulysses,
skimming the waves,
barely touching
that heroic existence
assigned to you without
your informed
and happy consent.

You are almost home,
get down
on your knees and kiss
the grit and sand of Ithaca.

THE POET AS HUSBAND

I write in a small shadowed corner
in order to bear light into the world,
though the light is not my own.
My darkness is no darkness to you
and nothing you should wish upon yourself,
but my light shall also be your light,
in which we shall see differently
but gloriously. I am not lame inside me,
no matter that I drag my foot, I have run here
through all my infirmities to bring you news
of a battle already won. Let my last breath
speak victory into the world. The race is run
and shall be run again, joyfully, and you shall
run with me, the territory opened
to us like returned laughter
or remembered childhood. Remember,
I was here, and you were here,
and together we made a world.

THE VOWS AT
GLENCOLMCILLE

It's as if the solid
green of the valley
were an island
held and bound
by the river flow
of stone
and when
in summer rain
white limestone
turns black
and the central green
is light-wracked
round the edges,
that dark
reflective gleam
of rock
becomes
an edging brilliance
that centers
a field
and makes us
see it
as deep emerald.

No other place
I know
speaks
simultaneously
of meadows
and desert,
absorbing dryness
and winter wet,
the ground
porous and forgiving
of all elements,
white and black,
wet and dry,
rich and barren,
like a human
marriage,
one hand
of welcome
raised,
the other
tightened
involuntary
on a concealed
knife in the
necessary
protections
of otherness.

As if someone
had said, you will
learn
in this land
the same welcome
and the same exile
as you do in your
mortal vows
to another,
you will promise
yourself
and abase yourself
and find yourself
again
in the intimacy
of opposites,
you will pasture yourself
in the living green
and the bare rock,
you will find
comfort in strangeness
and prayer
in aloneness,
you will be proud
and fierce
and single minded

even
in your unknowing
and you will
carry on
through all the seasons
of your living
and dying
until
your aloneness
becomes equal
to the trials
you have set yourself.

Then this land
will become again
the land
you imagined
when you saw it
for the first time
and these vows
of marriage
can become
again and again
the place you
make your
residence
like
this same
rough
intimate
and cradled
ground

between
stone horizons,
embracing
and also,
like the one
to whom
you made the vows,
always beyond you,
both utterly
with you
and both
strangely beautiful
to know
by their distance.

[IX]

SONS & DAUGHTERS

FIRST STEPS IN HAWKSHEAD CHURCHYARD

My son strode out into the world today,
twenty one steps on the grave of Ann Braithwaite,
her horizontal slab of repose, grey beneath
the lifting red socks, her exit from the world,
his entrance to the world of walking.

She must have lain beneath and smiled past
the small arms outstretched to the church tower of Hawkshead,
she must have borne him up, her help from the end of life
his beginning, her hands invisible, reaching to his.

He walked through each line explaining her life,
sixty two years by the small lake of Esthwaite,
lichen, green grass, grey walls and the falling
water of ice cold streams, his small place of play,
her mingling with the elements she lived with.

A meeting of two waters,
hers a deep pool, solitary in stillness,
his swift, bubbling from rock to rock,
pouring into her silence, a kingfisher
flare in her darkness, promise of light,

ineffable, unknowable, the touch of his feet
a promise of a world to come, solid on a life well lived.
His look of surprise when the church bell rang, her knowing.
The sound of time, his now, hers then. New rituals
are always played on the graves of those long dead.

BRENDAN

Jupiter in the western sky
and my
son walking
with the whole arc
of the sea behind him.

Above his head
the fishing pole
bent as if to catch
the day-lit star,
hovering
on the broad horizon.

The mere shape of him
in silhouette
I love so much.

The whip of his wrist
and rascal slant
of his cap

like some
hieroglyph
of love I deciphered
long ago
and read to myself
again and again.

When I first heard
him in the fluid darkness
before his birth,
calling to his mother and I
from the yet unknown
and unseen world
to which he belonged,

I could not know that
particular
slant of his
face or hand.
I could not know
how he would speak
to me.

Our love then was
for an unknown promise,

but just as strong
as if the promise was known.

May all our promises
from now
be just as strong
as they are hidden.

For no imagining could have
shaped you my boy
as I shape you now,
with the eyes of a fatherly
love that must be
shaped itself by your growing.

If I was asked
what my gift had been,
I should turn
to look at you.

You and your beloved
fishing pole,
casting for a star.

MY DAUGHTER ASLEEP

Carrying a child,
I carry a bundle of sleeping
future appearances.
I carry
my daughter adrift
on my shoulder,
dreaming her slender
dreams
and
I carry her
beneath
the window,
watching
her moon lit
palm
open
and close
like a tiny
folded
map,
each line
a path that leads
where I can't go,
so that I read her palm
not knowing
what I read

and
walk with her
in moon light
not knowing
with whom I walk,

making
invisible prayers
to go on
with her
where I can't
go,
conversing
with so many
unknowns
that must know her
more intimately
than I do.

And so to these
unspoken shadows
and this broad night
I make
a quiet
request
to the
great parental
darkness
to hold her
when I cannot,
to comfort her
when I am gone,
to help her learn
to love
the unknown
for itself,
to take it
gladly

like
a lantern
for the way
before her,
to make her see
where ordinary light
cannot help,
where happiness has fled,
where faith
will not reach.

My prayer tonight
for the great
and hidden
symmetries
of life
to reward this
faith I have
and twin
her passages
of loneliness
with friendship,
her exiles
with home coming,
her first awkward
steps with
promised onward
leaps.

May she find
in all this,
day or night,

the beautiful
centrality
of pure opposites,
may she discover
before she grows
old,
not to choose
so easily
between past
and present,
may she find
in
one or the other
her gifts
acknowledged.

And so
as I helped
to name her
I help to name
these
powers,
I bring
to life
what is needed,
I invoke
the help she'll
want
following
those moonlit lines
into a future
uncradled
by me
but

parented
by all
I call.

As she grows
away
from me,
may these life lines
grow with her,
keep her safe,
so
with my open palm
whose lines
have run before her
to make a safer way,
I hold her smooth cheek
and bless her
this night
and beyond it
and for every unknown
night to come.

[X]

THE VOICE

THE SOUL LIVES CONTENTED

The soul lives contented
by listening,
if it wants to change
into the beauty of
terrifying shapes,
it tries to speak.

That's why
you will not sing,
afraid as you are
of who might join with you.

The voice hesitant,
and her hand trembling
in the dark for yours.

She touches your face
and says your name
in the same instant.

The one you refused to say,
over and over,
the one you refused to say.

REVELATION MUST BE TERRIBLE

Revelation must be
   terrible with no time left
to say goodbye.

Imagine that moment,
   staring at the still waters,
with only the brief tremor

of your body to say
   you are leaving everything
and everyone you know behind.

Being far from home is hard, but you know,
   at least we are all exiled together.
When you open your eyes to the world

you are on your own for
   the first time. No one is
even interested in saving you now

and the world steps in
   to test the calm fluidity of your body
from moment to moment,

as if it believed you could join
   its vibrant dance
of fire and calmness and final stillness.

As if you were meant to be exactly
   where you are, as if,
like the dark branch of a desert river

you could flow on without a speck
   of guilt and everything
everywhere would still be just as it should be.

As if your place in the world mattered
   and the world could
neither speak nor hear the fullness of

its own bitter and beautiful cry
   without the deep well
of your body resonating in the echo.

Knowing that it takes only
   that first, terrible
word to make the circle complete,

revelation must be terrible
   knowing you can
never hide your voice again.

THE FIRE IN THE SONG

The mouth opens
   and fills the air
      with its vibrant shape,

until the air
   and the mouth
      become one shape.

And the first word,
   your own word,
      spoken from that fire,

surprises, burns,
   grieves you now
      because

you made that pact
   with a dark presence
      in your life.

He said, "If you only
   stop singing
      I'll make you safe."

And he repeated the line,
   knowing you would hear
      "I'll make you safe"

as the comforting
   sound of a door
      closed on the fear at last,

but his darkness crept
  under your tongue
    and became the dim

cave where
  you sheltered
    and you grew

in that small place
  too frightened to remember
    the songs of the world,

its impossible notes,
  and the sweet joy
    that flew out the door

of your wild mouth
  as you spoke.

THE SOUND OF THE WILD

Finally,
as the first firm
shadow
of evening
and
after many hours
falling toward
the body's
ebb and flow
of quiet revelation,

I hear that
voice
which belongs
to no one
except
the hidden
world
from which it flows
like a river,
filling the deep branches
of my body
with the wish to
slip beneath its quiet water
and disappear,

and listening
in the half light
beneath the
sound
of a single
brooding dove,

I try
to remember
my former life

and realize how quickly
the current travels
toward home,

how those
dark and irretrievable
blossoms of sound
I made in that time
have traveled
far-away
on the black surface
of memory

as if they no longer
belonged
to me.

As if my body might
feel lighter
without
their
weight
on what I have to say.

All night I followed
those currents
down to the sea
and finally
with that sweet
entangled
encouragement
we get
from greeting everything
we meet
along the way
as if we might
belong,

I sacrificed at the shores
of that great silence
my last possibility
for safety.

That's why I speak
the way I do.
I'm like everything else,
I have no immunity.

That's a fearful thing
to say
and having been there
you'll know
how much it means.

-We humans must be
such strange
and reluctant
creatures to live with.

All those cries
in the night
with which we could join,
the fox
crying *fox*

and those winged
and silent creatures
of the dusk

dropping with
such fierce delicacy
onto the shrew's
tremulous back.

Even when the owl
is silent
the shrew cries *owl*
into the black woods,
its life a last blaze
of sound
before the
small fire of its body
goes out.

Our own sounds
we refuse,
terrified as we are
to wake that voice
inside us,
waiting
with its wings folded
and its strange
expectant face.

The moment we try
to explain ourselves,
he moves those wings
to cover his face

and longs for
the wild
where cries
are involuntary things

and everybody
generously
gives their voice
to others,
even in their
last breath.

But this can be
no comfort,

knowing
the world
learns
the sound of its
own name
by dropping its
fearful weight
on us,
out of the dark,
when we least
expect,

so we can know the full
terror
of that love,

like the shrew
shrieking
its final gift—*owl!*

[XI]

FROM THE KAYAK

KAYAK I

The kayak
slips through a delicate channel
between islands,

this slight shape
cutting deep green,

for ten thousand years
the skin of
northern seals
nosing between ice floes,

now the russet glow
of orange fiberglass,
translucent,

floating at the edge
of evening,

until dark comes
and the paddle reaches
in the deep night
and dips between the Pleiades,

silently now
the kayak
nudges between stars.

KAYAK IV

From the northeast
undercurrents stirred by wind
ripple south
under the kayak
and with each rise
the boat lifts
to the dark clouds
covering Spieden,

with hips awash
and bow submerged,
each stroke
balanced on unseen pressures
lives for a moment
in the shoulders

and with the first sound
of indrawn breath,
the heart begins to flow
and become liquid,
spinning through the arms
like molten glass,

out here
life is a vibrant wire
pulled tight
between two opposing limbs

and it sings to the touch of the ocean.

KAYAK VI

When the mind lets go at last,
the kayak can roll with the waves,
following those green hillsides
to the very bottom.

And in each wave
pierced by the bow,
the rattling sound of raven bones
breaks into flowers
falling to the southeast.

In my arms
shapes enter from the air,
darken like the wings of a bird
then leave in the water.

In my voice,
I hear the old one waking at last,
calling the ravens
with spume-filled wings
in and out of the chest.

His body is hardened by cold,
when the sun breaks through,
salt
sparkles from his back.

His hands have crushed
and thrown across the water
the ashes of his campfires
so that each place he leaves
floats out before him
and everywhere
he finds the places he has left
renewed like the ashes
lifted and scattered in the wind.

Even here
paddling the purple line
where inland water meets ocean
and light sweeps the mind clean,
we find a place to be together
– old friends after long parting –
a final campfire
as the sun goes down.

Others look to find us
what do they see?

Two white stumps,
bleached by the sun
where the waves come in.

OUT ON THE OCEAN

In these waves
I am caught on shoulders
lifting the sky,

each crest
breaks sharply
and suddenly rises,

in each steep wall
my arms work in the strong movement
of other arms,

the immense energy
each wave throws up with hand outstretched
grabs the paddle,

the blades flash
lifting veils of spray as the bow rears
terrified, then falls.

With five miles to go
of open ocean
the eyes pierce the horizon

the kayak pulls round
like a pony held by unseen reins
shying out of the ocean

and the spark behind fear,
recognized as life,
leaps into flame.

★

Always this energy smoulders inside,
when it remains unlit,
the body fills with dense smoke.

WATCHING THE SUN GO DOWN

In the evening, that shadow on Coldspring
is where the sun goes down.
Time, when the bow touches shore, to watch
the sun roll down that long curve of hillside
and wait.

Paddle laid crossways,
back leaning on the upright seat,
heels resting in cold water,
rudder pulled up.

Time to feel the day long movement of the paddle
come to rest in tired arms,
to lift the spray-skirt, stand up,
keep the weight low,
step out of the boat
into the shallows.

Time to pull the kayak up the beach,
open the hatches, take out the tent,
turn the kayak over,
on the rough grey drift-wood logs.

Time to say nothing, just watch,
without moving, without sound,
the sun reflected, shimmering,

setting on fire
the white length of an upturned kayak.

SETTING OUT AT DUSK

The kayak sits on the black water
covered by trees.
Late October leaves drift by its bow.

Paddling out for weekend days away from noise
this silence leaves me unsure,
an old friend I haven't met for years.

I sit, rudder pulled up, getting to know him,
double bladed paddle
dipping slowly in cold water

and looking up, see a single otter, skittering
on the grassy bank, stop,
—look round, see me, low shape on still water,—

roll back into the trees, leave me with silence.
I watch clouds gather between islands,
the wind pick up, shearwaters lift on the grey sea.

Through the sip-slap of waves on the lifting hull
I prick my ears for the small sounds
at the very edge of silence and then,

I pull the bow out into the wide sea,
paddle dipping
toward darkness and enter again. The quiet.

TEN YEARS LATER

When the mind is clear
and the surface of the now still,
now swaying water

slaps against
the rolling kayak,

I find myself near darkness,
paddling again to Yellow Island.

Every spring wildflowers
cover the grey rocks.

Every year the sea breeze
ruffles the cold and lovely pearls
hidden in the center of the flowers

as if remembering them
by touch alone.

A calm and lonely, trembling beauty
that frightened me in youth.

Now their loneliness
feels familiar, one small thing
I've learned these years,

how to be alone,
and at the edge of aloneness
how to be found by the world.

Innocence is what we allow
to be gifted back to us
once we've given ourselves away.

There is one world only,
the one to which we gave ourselves
utterly, and to which one day

we are blessed to return.

[XII]

ALBION

THERE ARE THOSE

There are those we know
buried
not far beneath this green land
with whom
we have not spoken for a long time,
who remember
what we have forgotten.

One day they will speak again,
surprised at their own voices
singing the old song,
how the earth is given and taken,
how the world will come again.

And we who also listen surprised,
will come again to the land of lands.
Our own, the place we've chosen,
after the false start
and the slouching toward
falseness.

And find ourselves on the old roads
but new, walking with Blake, head up,
toward Jerusalem.

COTSWOLD

A sandstone grave crowding shellfish,
fossils crusted round a copper plaque.

A silent church and an old house
and small green lines explaining grief.

The quiet rivulets of centuries,
the stone green moss of years gone by,

the green hillsides, stone gold walls, shadows,
the buried pathways in the quiet wood.

Water falling enlivens, greens,
soaks and comes together underground.

Earth rising meets, moulds, holds,
holds on to what it owns, takes back

nothing not given. Over the shoals
of leaves and humus, over the branch

of oak and hedgerow, over the white aproned
hawthorn holding her skirts in the wind,

in the still moments before the wind shivers
across the still reflection on the moss rimmed pond,

the white clouded sky is sailing as ever,
over the rook-nests in the eastern woods.

And this lane that I follow, burying through
greensward and the grey limbs of trees,

shadowing the rutted track into silence,
is no place to speak. Now for years gone by

this entanglement of green has grown to
this moment's walking as if to measure

my readiness for quiet. Where I've failed
before now my body's alive to enter the silent

reflection of water from last night's rain,
filling the wheel tracks in the muddy lane.

Walking the roads is enough today,
I'll follow the dark line of receding sun

over by Edgeworth, drop down, keep to the hedgerows,
speak only to myself, find myself speechless

at the edge of night. Composing clear lines,
-everything I've seen the tongue can tell.

HARTSHEAD

In Hartshead I'm walking paths I've walked for years,
following the line of trees through wind, rain

and dark clouds moving fast from the moors. I've learned
to know since young the faint path through the fields

that takes you to the woods, above the valley,
leads you through hedgerows spiked with haws.

And still between those trees I see Huddersfield
cramped in the Colne, Castle Hill, the westering line

of Saddleworth Moor smouldering above. Winter's bleak
but still there's the green armchair of the valley sheltered

by wood and the pale green fields worked from the farm.
In snow, there's a sharp edge to the eye's inventory of

stonewall and hedgerow, a white silence stretched to breaking
on the still days the wind begs off from the west.

Spring's an apple green, bladed with new grass and blackened
with cows turned out from the barns. The hawthorn's white

surprise still shocks the eye's forgetful winter rest. Summer's
a still image. Shimmering heat and the streaked blur of a rabbit

out from the gorse on Hartshead lane. The road a parched wander
to liquid, waist-high green-gold barley foresting the path

to the Grey Ox Inn. Now Autumn's the damped fire of fallen leaves
raked over by wind, the earthly crackle of bracken underfoot,

the giver of vision, the light defined by dark, the firm upward needle
of Clifton spire flared by a single ray from the clouds.

YORKSHIRE

I love the dead
and their quiet living
underground
and I love the rain
on my face.

And in childhood,
I loved the wind
on the moors
that carried the rain
and that carried the ashes
of the dead,
like a spring sowing
of memory,
stored through all
the winters past.

In the dark November
onset of the winter
in which I was born,
I was set down in the
folds of that land
as if I belonged there,
and in that first night
under the evening shadow
of the moors and most likely
with the wind in the west,
as it would be for most
of my growing life,

I was breathing in the tang
and troubles of that immense
and shadowing sky
as I was breathing the shadows
of my mother's body,
learning who and what was close
and how I could belong.

What great and
abstract power
lent me to those
particularities
I cannot know
but body
and soul were made
for that belonging.

Yorkshire is as hard
as a spade-edge
but the underpinnings
of the people and the land
in which we lived,
flowed and turned like the
river I knew in my valley.
The blunt solidity of my elders
floated like mountains
on the slow but fluid lava
of their history.

But on this solid yet floating
land I must have been
as Irish as my mother
and amid the straight certainties
of my father's Yorkshire,
I felt beneath the damp moor's
horizon the curved invisible
lines that drew everything
together, the underground stream
of experience that could not
be quarried or brought to the surface
but only dowsed, felt, followed
or intuited from above.

Poetry then became the key, my way
underground into what was hidden
by the inept but daily coverings
of grown-up surface speech.
Something sacred in the land
was left unsaid in people's mouths
but was written into our inheritance
and that small volume of Thom Gunn's
youthful poetry from
the library's high tiptoe shelf
was the angel's gift to me.
Opened and read in my
young boy's hands,
it revealed the first code
I sought and needed to begin
speaking what I felt
had been forgotten.

Full stretch I reached again
along the spines and touched
another, *other* life, pulling
down into my hands
The Hawk in the Rain.
Ted Hughes' dark book full of northern omens
hovering above my
own child's shadow on the ground,
my heart and mind
caught in those written claws
and whisked into the sky.
The first rush of poetry's
extended arms a complete
abduction of my person.

That was the beginning.
The first line on the open page
of my new life, the rest
would be more difficult
but that was the soil in which
I would grow, and that was the
life *into* which I would grow,
blessed and badgered by the northern
sweeps of light and dark
and the old entanglements
to which I was born. Always
on the wuthering moors
the gifts and stories and poetry
of the unknown and unvisited dead
who brought their history
to the world in which I grew.

Orphaned by poetry
from my first home,
to find a greater home
out in the world,
I wandered from that land
and began to write
youthfully and insubstantially,
slowly making myself
real and seeable by writing
myself into an original world
which had borne and
grown me so generously.

Belonging to one old land
so much by birth,
I learn each day now
what it means to
be born into a new land
and new people. The open
moor of the American
mind, gusted and shaken
by imagined new worlds
and imagined new clouds
and the fears and griefs of
the peopled and unknowable distances
of a vast land, and still amidst
everything, an innocence
which survives here untouched
amidst a difficult inheritance.

Let my history then
be a gate unfastened
to a new life
and not a barrier
to my becoming.
Let me find the ghosts
and histories and barely
imagined future
of this world,
and let me now have
the innocence to grow
just as well in shadow or light
by what is gifted
in this land
as the one to which I was born.

[XIII]
IRELAND

HANDS ACROSS THE WATER

Impossible to write about Ireland: –
the blood's entangled and the heart won't go
where others went before me,
shaking their swords and their pens at the moon.

Whatever brought my mother to England,
banished her son to the dark glass of distance.

I remember cards from the family:-
and the well formed lines
"Hands across the water."

Marvellous cliché worth singing again!
and I harbored those words
as a wry link with home.

Now I know the short-cropped grass
on the high Reeks of Kerry,
the cold grey water
in the Blasket Sound.

And down at the Mile Post
out of Waterford town,
my great-uncle Davy,
coming to meet,
ducking and weaving,
arms flexed in a boxer's crook.

"Did you see the fight last night?
The best in all my years;
they stood there,
fist to fist,
arm to arm,
knee to knee,
and toe to toe
and by God,
they murdered one another."

Hands across the water
well enough;
but now I'm forever
wrapped in its arms
crouched,
trying to break,
shielding my face
from the welcoming blows.

RETURN

The day started with a flurry of gulls
and a single cry, as if I had spoken
and out of the deep cave where my tongue lies,
birds were scattering in an open sky.

I went to the rail and watched them rise
over the grey clouds as if the sky were a sea
and the sea was cold now, full of shapes
and the horse-tails of winter.

And I spoke, involuntary,
out of a delighted mouth,
the old, strange word,

Ireland;
joy when uttered, grief when heard.

SPIDDAL HARBOUR 1976

It is night.
Three fishermen
treading softly
on the cool wet stones,
carry a tray of shining fish.

The youngest stops,
looks out to sea,
murmurs in a low voice
while the others pull him on.

"I am sick of this life,
I should have gone with Michael
- to America."

They will not look at him,
they will not turn,
but the moon looks at him
and the fish
with each, silver, upturned eye.

SEEKING OUT TIME

In Ireland, Time has never been understood.
Each day under brooding clouds
the rocks come ashore on the coast of Clare.
They find Time, a silhouette, dark and indistinct,
a black bird perching in the hedgerows.

They seek Time out, want to know what he's doing,
why history lies thick on the ground
like braided rope, gold, satin,
wound with the blood of men and women,
tight knots choking the first spring grass.

Time stays at a distance, but they move closer.
His song whistles as if from a cave
whose entrance is Clouds-parting.
His yellow beak catches the sun
and his black feathers turn blue in the changing light.

Time goes mute, they are rocks from the sea,
unknown, forbidding, before Time.
His eyes smoulder, their small veins branching,
filling with blood. Why should rocks come ashore?

Time takes off, begins to creep
his wings across the hills, makes darkness
all day long, a sky of feathers on which,
head tilted sideways, his eye becomes a strange moon.

They shake their fists, threaten him,
but Time has risen, covered in twilight
like dust, no one can touch him.

Time sends down mist, chaos by night, startled curses,
screams that appear from their own throats.
"Time is afraid" they taunt.
Time says, "I am friends with no one."

He will not come down. They began to sing.
Slowly they form in a circle and slowly
they chant the song of the shoreline,
filling the cave of his wings with sound.
Bringing Time down.

Slowly he descends and slowly he curves in the song.
The breeze softens his feathers,
his eyes glaze toward the prison at their center.

Time comes down, stoops right in their center.
His beak curves to the brown earth,
when it touches, his eyes flash fire, cold and clear.
Time leaves Ireland, disappears and leaves them,
frozen, standing stones on the bare hill.

POEM IN PRAISE OF THE TRINITY HARP

For Peter Kilroy

Rough barked, walnut brown, milky darkness,
shaped like a wind blown tree,
etched and hieroglyphed, a calligraphy of shapes and love.

Three branches of willow
held together by strong arms
invisible inside the wood, waiting for other arms.

Worn, round, rubbed where the left arm stretched down
and where the eye descends we find below
low, where the right arm touched, this valley of use,

glen of embracement, erotic hollow of summer delight.
Here the crooked arm held,
here the sounds like small green buds, grew into leaf,

rustled with wind, filled with sound from the western sea
a dark forest of notes rushing inland
to the fields, filling the heartland of Ireland.

And this tree leans, the whole tree leans in the wind
of centuries, swayed by time and the downward
pull of brass, gold sinews snapping between opposites.

Even after the wind, in silence, among books, it has a voice,
in the fields near Kenmare I heard it,
a song full of grief, an utterance of curlews, a single drop

of rain sibilating to the ground when the storm had passed.
Whoever sat behind this frame
was master of that quiet, brought music from nothing,

felt the strength of the tree itself, passing
the pulse of the air to his wrists,
turning his hands to the blurred gold of strings.

Power like this yet it cannot stand by itself.
It needs the forward lean, the crooked arms,
the face warmed by firelight, the listening.

So much strength to need the arms of the weak!
So much affection to stop its falling,
to hold it warmly, snugged to the shoulder.

To feel, between the last string and the forepillar
that fierce and impenetrable curve
where we know the sound was sown as though it were a seed.

To know as we hear it, the exact place the sound rested
as it grew inside the ear
and became a tree again, waiting for the ear to waken

to the first impossible note
until silence grew on the tree
and with glad hands we plucked its fruit from the wild air.

THE HORSE WHISPERER

Ireland's the ghost-horse
all right,
rearing out of history
like the wraith-herd seen
at Fanore.

After the events
of Bloody Sunday,
and after the peace
thrown away,
and the guns still hidden,
and the red hand
taking the ghostly reins again,
we saw the tiny twinkled
lights of violence
from every townland.

Looked in the lamp of
one another's
eyes, felt that
animal presence
riding the
night fields again and the
encroaching loss
of control in the village
that we knew heralded
the ancient panic.

So now they were waiting
in the autumn rain,
as they used to wait,
by the crossroads,
gathered on both sides
to see what was anticipated
to be a miracle,
though at first, everyone averted
their eyes from what they
knew to be, in these times, too old
and too innocent a magic
to believe in.

The beast
somehow caught
and led between
everyone
and the man waiting
in the hushed hysteria.

His mouth moving
close to the ghost ear,
they saw a hand pass over
the twitched shoulder
and felt the first
frightened shudder of the horse
pass back through the crowd,
like a wave breaking.

"For Christ's sake
give him room."

Then they strained to hear
what they knew could
not be heard,
in the silence they

could only wait,
their split hypnotic faith
now joined involuntary
as they watched
the calmed violence
fall away,
caught in the animal body
of his first word.

TIANANMEN
(The Man in Front of the Tank)

On the way from Kenmare
I remember the old man
at the roadside,
his casual thumb following
the lane's curve
for the length of a hillside.
Shopping bags leant
against his knees, the two circles
jutting with milk, sugar, tea,
half a loaf of oat bread
cut straight down the middle.

The one hand lifted in thanks
and the other tipped to the cap's edge
before he dropped it to the door handle,
lifted his bags into the back
and took his seat in the car.
That easy lack of obligation
in the swing and pitch of the bags
hitting the back seat.
I sensed in him his far-west
inheritance passed down the long
centuries of rain and cold wind,
into his body. I felt how easily
he belonged, coming out of any
weather, rain or shine
to the stranger's hospitality.

Just after the close of the door
you could smell the cut grass
on him, the well worn wool,
and the faint breath of porter.

(My great-uncle Davy
coming in from the garden,
though never the porter,
teetotal now for fifty years)

But the familiar Sunday smell
was on me now and
I drove slowly,
matching the long ease
of the miles he'd walked
from the country shop.

At the final curve of the hill
and in the keen wind
above his fields,
we hit the swaying light-swept land,
the patchwork of leaning walls,
the scrub, the scruff and the rusted gates,
and at the farm track's end,
found his cottage,
the walls a cracked gray
spider's web edged by blue.

I walked in with him then for the
proffered tea. The oiled tablecloth
puddled with sugar and rimed with
cup rings, in the corner by the
cracked sink a television pulled
round on the draining board.

Above the sink a shattered
window pane, and beyond, a curlew
spiralling over the green barley.

He sat me down and set
the kettle on the blue gas flame
talked of his son
and when he might come back
to these broken walls.
"Set them straight, by God."

I thought of loneliness,
how it works at the edge
of all experience.

He filled the teapot,
set down the milk jug,
the sugar, the cups,
rattling the saucers
with a shaking hand.

About to say something
more, the name of his son
half-formed on his lips,
he stopped himself
and looking round
for a help that was not present,
jabbed the television's
waiting button.

I waited one half second
for the particular
unwanted and distant
form of oblivion we were
about to join on the screen.
I preferred silence,
conversation, and the view
through the cracked window,

when suddenly the image of
a great crowd and tumult,
and in the kitchen something
ancient between us recognized
the hysteria of confrontation and
at the other end of the distant square,
an enormous emptiness.

A line of tanks was pushing
slowly into the emptiness,
as if working through a
pliant powerful barrier,
but there was only a single man
holding them back,
his silhouette leaning forward
as if bowing to the tank.

The old man's hand shook
holding the pot
and the thick black tea scalded
my outstretched hand.

My wrist came fast and involuntary
to my mouth and I bit the glowing welt
pushing my tongue against the heat.

But I couldn't take my eyes
from the man in front of the tank,
his head bowed but unmoving,
as if confronting at last,
the god hidden in the metal altar.

The old man stood stock still,
then turned, looked at me,
my scalded hand,
the screen, the young man in front
of the tank. His eyes narrowed.
His faced changed
to a helpless fury. "There's a picture
for the whole fecking century,
my son's out in the world
and God knows what he's standing
in front of now, but whatever it is,
Jesus Christ, look at these fields
he'll never come back
and why should he?"

THE ALL OF IT

For Des Lally

This book-lined perspective
whose vanishing point
lies in the thin air
somewhere
beyond the window.

These loved words with no
home in the world
without being read,
found now in a field,
now on the broad mountain
or in the sky
traveling beyond us.

And us amongst the books
talking up an edge
between the past
and all
that's bound to be said
when the story's told.

The river below all the while,
giving out from the lake
where the salmon leap,
leaving the mountain

for those who live in it
and those who live by it,
all of us met by the flow
and all of us
in the end
left in its wake.

Ourselves at the edge,
following the lapse and steal
of the water, trying
to catch the risen meaning
as it goes, no more
and no less,
that's
the all of it.

DUN AENGUS

And when you go, try to go before Easter,
taking the *Queen of Aran* from Rossaveal,
out to the island when the wind is fresh
and the rain still cold and the fires still bright
in the harbour pubs. Then rent yourself
a bike from Michael Mullen who stands
there where the pier first meets the land
so there's no need for conversation
along the gusty road except the one
you hold balanced between
the wind on one side and the ocean
on the other. At that time, March has yet
to lose its edge and somehow
the roads still hold the history
of winter's easy quiet
and somewhere at the back of it all
and out of the west, you can hear
each clear invisible voice
speaking to you distinct and whole,
giving you the full inheritance
as you ride along the *Boreen Oir*
in the teeth of the wind, your eyes wet
with the searching cold until you can see it
above you and to the left, brooding
on the cliff edge. Don't stop
to layer your mind with
the necessities of history but walk
without looking to right or left,
straight through the glass lit exhibit
guarding the path like
a somnolent post-modern dragon
about to ensnare you
and break the clean,

airy, outside approach
but plough straight on,
leaving your bike to stand
below while you take the path at a full
walk, impatient to reach the edge above,
cradled by the curving walls, crawling
the last few feet to the unfenced edge
where the sea's a tilted table swelling
against the rocks three hundred feet below
and the snow isn't snow
but the upward spume from breaking waves
and your mind isn't your own
but a troubling of edge and current,
going this way and that, as if you were
both fluid and substantial,
alone in this world,
and communal with all horizons,
an airy something and a solid witness,
a visitation and a disappearance,
someone made up of neither
regrets nor anticipation
but a ghost of other ghosts, a visitor
at the cliff edge of history, hearing
in the voice torn away in the wind,
a blowing away, a first promise,
a shouted pledge for the year to come.

THE SEVEN STREAMS

Come down drenched, at the end of May,
with the cold rain so far into your bones
that nothing will warm you
except your own walking
and let the sun come out at the day's end
by Slievenaglasha with the rainbows doubling
over Mulloch Mor and see your clothes
steaming in the bright air. Be a provenance
of something gathered, a summation of
previous intuitions, let your vulnerabilities
walking on the cracked, sliding limestone,
be this time, not a weakness, but a faculty
for understanding what's about
to happen. Stand above the Seven Streams,
letting the deep down current surface
around you, then branch and branch
as they do, back into the mountain,
and as if you were able for that flow,
say the few necessary words
and walk on, broader and cleansed
for having imagined.

MAMEEN

Be infinitesimal under that sky, a creature
even the sailing hawk misses, a wraith
among the rocks where the mist parts slowly.

Recall the way mere mortals are overwhelmed
by circumstance, how great reputations
dissolve with infirmity and how you,
in particular, stand a hairsbreadth from losing
everyone you hold dear.

Then, look back down the path to the north,
the way you came, as if seeing
your entire past and then south
over the hazy blue coast as if present
to a broad future.

Remember the way you are all possibilities
you can see and how you live best
as an appreciator of horizons,
whether you reach them or not.

Admit that once you have got up
from your chair and opened the door,
once you have walked out into the clean air
toward that edge and taken the path up high
beyond the ordinary, you have become
the privileged and the pilgrim,
the one who will tell the story
and the one, coming back
from the mountain,
who helped to make it.

TOBAR PHADRAIC

Turn sideways into the light as they say
the old ones did and disappear
into the originality of it all.

Be impatient with easy explanations
and teach that part of the mind
that wants to know everything
not to begin questions it cannot answer.

Walk the green road above the bay
and the low glinting fields
toward the evening sun, let that Atlantic
gleam be ahead of you and the gray light
of the bay below you, until you catch,
down on your left, the break in the wall,
for just above in the shadows
you'll find it hidden, a curved arm
of rock holding the water close to the mountain,
a just-lit surface smoothing a scattering of coins,
and in the niche above, notes to the dead
and supplications for those who still live.

But for now, you are alone with the transfiguration
and ask no healing for your own
but look down as if looking through time,
as if through a rent veil from the other
side of the question you've refused to ask.

And you remember now, that clear stream
of generosity from which you drank,
how as a child your arms could rise and your palms
turn out to touch the blessing of the world.

COLEMAN'S BED

Make a nesting now, a place to which
the birds can come, think of Kevin's
prayerful palm holding the blackbird's egg
and be the one, looking out from this place
who warms interior forms into light.
Feel the way the cliff at your back
gives shelter to your outward view,
then bring from those horizons
all discordant elements that seek a home.

Be taught now, among the trees and rocks,
how the discarded is woven into shelter,
learn the way things hidden and unspoken
slowly proclaim their voice in the world.
Find that far inward symmetry
to all outward appearances, apprentice
yourself to yourself, begin to welcome back
all you sent away, be a new annunciation,
make yourself a door through which
to be hospitable, even to the stranger in you.

See with every turning day,
how each season makes a child
of you again, wants you to become
a seeker after rainfall and birdsong,
watch how it weathers you to a testing
in the tried and true, tells you
with each falling leaf, to leave and slip away,
even from the branch that held you,
to go when you need to, to be courageous,
to be like a last word you'd want to say
before you leave the world.

Above all, be alone with it all,
a hiving off, a corner of silence
amidst the noise, refuse to talk,
even to yourself, and stay in this place
until the current of the story
is strong enough to float you out.

Ghost then, to where others
in this place have come before,
under the hazel, by the ruined chapel,
below the cave where Coleman slept,
become the source that makes
the river flow, and then the sea
beyond. Live in this place
as you were meant to and then,
surprised by your abilities,
become the ancestor of it all,
the quiet, robust and blessed Saint
that your future happiness
will always remember.

[XIV]
HIMALAYA

MUKTINATH

Dawn at Muktinath
and I look through the window,
white mountains and the steady
slopes of snow,
cold scent of pine and the raven-call
of black birds
circling upward - toward nothing.

So the breath escapes the mouth,
spiralling in a cold room,
so the words leave our lips,
the first line of a long poem
with no courage to finish.

This is the place the path begins,
the empty room beneath the breath
where everything we've broken
comes back to be repaired,
where bitterness returns, opens,
turns to a final sourness
on the lime-washed walls
and disappears.

This is the place we start again,
place sunburnt knuckles in moist eyes
and bow the head
feel the rough cold wall
on the forehead and weep.

This is the place we stop,
look up, lean out the window
and find the first signs of life.

Beneath us
a child is crying,
while above,
a tight arrow of driven ponies
points the way to the high pass.

TILICHO LAKE

In this high place
    it is as simple as this,
        leave everything you know behind.

Step toward the cold surface,
    say the old prayer of rough love
        and open both arms.

Those who come with empty hands
    will stare into the lake astonished,
        there, in the cold light
            reflecting pure snow

        the true shape of your own face.

THE FACES AT BRAGA

In monastery darkness
by the light of one flashlight,
the old shrine room waits in silence.

While above the door,
we see the terrible figure,
fierce eyes demanding, "Will you step through?"

And the old monk leads us,
bent back nudging blackness,
prayer beads in the hand that beckons.

We light the butter lamps
and bow, eyes blinking in the
pungent smoke, look up without a word,

see faces in meditation,
a hundred faces carved above,
eye lines wrinkled in the hand held light.

Such love in solid wood!
Taken from the hillsides and carved in silence,
they have the vibrant stillness of those who made them.

Engulfed by the past
they have been neglected, but through
smoke and darkness they are like the flowers

we have seen growing
through the dust of eroded slopes,
their slowly opening faces turned toward the mountain.

Carved in devotion
their eyes have softened through age
and their mouths curve through delight of the carver's hand.

If only our own faces
would allow the invisible carver's hand
to bring the deep grain of love to the surface.

If only we knew
as the carver knew, how the flaws
in the wood led his searching chisel to the very core,

we would smile too
and not need faces immobilized
by fear and the weight of things undone.

When we fight with our failing
we ignore the entrance to the shrine itself
and wrestle with the guardian, fierce figure on the side of good.

And as we fight
our eyes are hooded with grief
and our mouths are dry with pain.

If only we could give ourselves
to the blows of the carver's hands,
the lines in our faces would be the trace lines of rivers

feeding the sea
where voices meet, praising the features
of the mountain, and the cloud, and the sky.

Our faces would fall away,
until we, growing younger toward death
every day, would gather all our flaws in celebration,

to merge with them perfectly,
impossibly, wedded to our essence,
full of silence from the carver's hands.

DREAMING AT BRAGA

Two miles to go and the door will open,
-three old men round an open fire.
One offers rice and one offers *dahl*
and the third asks fiercely
with empty hands,
"Oh which, traveller, is the true I?"

BED BUGS IN KAGBENI

Cold morning on a strange bed,
suddenly I am not alone!
Sharing the warmth inside my sleeping bag
there are small beings!
And I, lovingly, like Avolokitesvara,
great bodisattva of compassion,
gaze down upon them.
Strange heads and many legs!
Sharp and searching horns for human hair!

At times like this, we abandon our search for meaning,
take the bag outside, hang it on the high wall,
inside out, look at the mountain, high snow
reflecting pure light all down the valley, onto the bag.

Go inside, wash, drink hot tea with salt
and small spots of yak butter.
Eat flat breads baked in pine-ash,
come out refreshed.
Take the bag, now unpopulated, in both hands,
lift it to the nose.
Fragrance of new morning!

Pack it away, go out the doors with friends
who also shared the night with others.
Ask how they slept,
laugh,
on the steep road to Jarkhot.

A WOMAN'S VOICE

Night at Latamarang.
Above the river and call of cicadas
I remember old words and old bonds
and beneath the singing of a woman's voice,
the sight of my mother's face.

How strange to have forgotten!
The young boy with eyes wide,
the woman's cheek so close,
the small hand held up to be taken,
the yearning filled, the sun-warmed sky,
the mountain solid, immovable,
even here in the Himalaya
a thousand Buddhas of compassion,
carved in the steep rocks above,
bow down before the mother-love.

The teaching came with me,
the cicadas stop their calling,
the starry sky has turned to calm,
the river runs in the steep valley
to the dry lands and the waiting sea.

Years ago now I remember
I put away that guiding hand
to find the way myself
and find, strange wonder,
at journey's end
and with another strength,
the self-same hand again.

THIS POEM A PRAYER FLAG

This poem a prayer flag.
Almost written—then gone.
The wind—I cannot touch it!

TAKSTANG

Takstang monastery,
the tiger's nest.

Two thousand feet
to the valley floor.

After many days
alone in the mountains,

the body hesitates
at the sight of a single roof.

Having listened to the wind,
sufficient to itself,

like a single clear breath
from the body of the mountain,

we hear the sutra's
diamond hard presence

at the center of experience
so clearly now,

spoken from the felt rhythm
of a ten-day walk.

And having crossed the pass
in cold rain,

we wait, about to ripen
into our own going.

Like a drop of clear water
hanging from the cliff edge,

its own transparent world
growing from within,

until it fills with just enough
to flow on

out of the mountains
as we do.

So silent now, only the sound,
as we go

of that pure water
falling

toward home.

THE OLD INTERIOR ANGEL

Young, male and
immortal as I was,
I stopped at the first sight
of that broken bridge.

The taut cables snapped
and the bridge planks
concertina-ed
into a crazy jumble
over the drop,
four hundred feet
to the craggy   •
stream.

I sat and watched
the wind shiver
on the broken planks,
as if by looking hard
and long enough,
the life-line
might spontaneously
repair itself,
–but watched in vain.

An hour I sat
in silence,
checking each
involuntary movement
of the body toward
that trembling
bridge
with a fearful mind,
and an emphatic
shake of the head.

Finally, facing defeat
and about to go back
the way I came
to meet the others.

Three days round
by another pass.

Enter the old mountain woman
with her stooped gait,
her dark clothes
and her dung basket
clasped to her back.

Small feet shuffling
for the precious
gold-brown
fuel for cooking food.

Intent on the ground
she glimpsed my feet
and looking up
said "Namaste"
"I greet the God in you"
the last syllable
held like a song.

I inclined my head
and clasped my hands
to reply, but
before I could look up,
she turned her lined face
and went straight across
that shivering chaos
of wood
and broken steel
in one movement.

One day the hero
sits down,
afraid to take
another step,
and the old interior angel
limps slowly in
with her no-nonsense
compassion
and her old secret
and goes ahead.

"Namaste"
you say
and follow.

STATUE OF BUDDHA

Your hand moves
in the gesture of welcome.
Your lips in the gestures of praise.

You believed in your own sound
and so everything you said
is still being spoken.

In that first step
away from home
you came so far, and all alone,
faithful to all things
as you met them
until finally everything
bowed to you
and everything spoke to you
in its own voice.

You were the child
whose first step
encompassed the four directions.
You said,
"Heaven above, earth below,
I alone and sacred."

Creation means
finding the new world
in that first
fierce step,
with no thought of return.

THE STATUE OF SHIVA

The statue of Shiva
entwined with his lover
– the way
we love to hold closely
what is ours.

Their speech
so plain to the attentive ear
bowing close to listen

"The universe refuses the vows
of the celibate.
Preparing them instead with
songs for their marriage.
Everything it knows
was born of the great embrace."

[XV]

THOSE I KNOW
AND HAVE KNOWN

NEWS OF DEATH

For Tom Charlotte

Last night they came with news of death,
not knowing what I would say.

I wanted to say,
"The green wind is running through the fields,
making the grass lie flat."

I wanted to say,
"The apple blossom flakes like ash,
covering the orchard wall."

I wanted to say,
"The fish float belly up in the slow stream,
stepping stones to the dead."

They asked if I would sleep that night,
I said I did not know.

For this loss I could not speak,
the tongue lay idle in a great darkness,
the heart was strangely open,
the moon had gone,
and it was then
when I said, "He is no longer here,"
that the night put its arm around me
and all the white stars turned bitter with grief.

TAN-Y-GARTH

Elegy for Michael

This grass-grown hill's a patchwork lined with walls
I've grown to love. Four hundred years at least the

hill farm's clung tenacious to the weathered slope,
over the Ogwen and the green depths of Mon.

The eye has weathered also, into the grey rocks
and the fields bright with spring, the wind blown light

from the mountain, filling the valley,
the low backed sheep following the fence,

hemmed by dogs and John's crooked staff, the still valley
filled with his shouts and the mewling of sheep pressed

through the gate. Beneath Yr Elen, the bowl of Llafer's
stirred with mist, the dogs lie low in the tufted grass and

watch with pure intent, the ragged back of the last sheep
entering the stone-bound pen. The rough ground of Wales

lives in the mind for years, springing moor grass under
feet treading concrete, hundreds of miles from home,

and the ground has names, songs full of grief, sounds
that belong to a single stream, Caseg's the place of the mare,

Cwm Llafer's the valley of speech, utterance of wind,
Fryddlas the blue moorland filled by the sky. The farm

passed down but never possessed lives father to son,
life after life, feeding the sheep with grass,

the people with sheep and memory with years
lived looking at mountains. One single glance of a hillside

darkened by cloud is enough to sense the world it breathes
and the names need all the breath we have-

Carnedd Llewellyn, Carnedd Dafydd, Garnedd Uchaf, all the
Carneddau, Yr Elen of the shining light, Drosgl the endless

ridge curving to nothing. One man I know loved this place so
much he said he'd found his place to die. Years I knew him

here, walking the high moor lines or watching the coals
of a winter fire in the cottage grate. And die he did, but not

before one month's final joy in wild creation gave him that
full sight he'd glimpsed in Blake, he too struggled with his angel,

in and out of hospital, the white sheets and clouds unfolded
to the mountain's bracing sense of space, now he was ready,

his heart so long at the edge of the nest shook its
wings and flew into the hills he loved. Became the hills

he loved. Walked with an easy rest cradled by the faith he
nursed for years in doubt. His ashes are scattered over by

Aber, the water continually saying his name, as I still go
home to Tan-y-Garth speaking the names of those I know.

EDWARD

Aquiline, yet youthful, resembling
still the photograph you showed me
of the father I could never meet,
I see your face now set against
the evening glow of hills.
Your lit profile to me, well-loved
and familiar, like each
Cumbrian crag and steep
to which I brought you that
first summer of our friendship.

I hear your laugh now in the quiet
dark of a fellside, our limbs tired
from a thousand feet of rock
and summer heat, the gold light
of fireflies haunting the trees below
and the ground's embracing
warmth like a loving dream,
no talk but the sound of our feet
on the quiet path to the valley floor.

We live in the shadow of those
memories as we sometimes live
in the shadow of those with
extraordinary gifts. Sometimes the days
are generous and miraculous in what
they can bestow and sometimes
a life must be measured
against a certain remembered epoch,
when the veil between heaven and earth

was thin as gossamer and the shared
experience close to the angels,
for I felt our winged flight
above the valley floors,
roped in one another's care,
brought us to that earned necessity
which we look back to
and name as love, and we
know now that out of that towered
landscape of rock and cascading fell,
we forged our friendship for a lifetime.

Each warm summer then for years
we'd take the long drive north
talking together, letting speech
and renewed friendship merge
the year we'd spent apart,
our voices warm and our eyes
following the sun's low track in the
evening sky, until our stories grew
darker and quieter like the evening ground,
and the shape of those hills
once more resembled the silhouette
of our familiar and imagined arrival.

Our silence in the car by then,
a pure anticipation of that heaven
of grey and lichened stone to which
we drove. The dormant and sleeping
ropes of perlon coiled in the back,
waiting to be unwound into the upper light
of a Cumbrian cliff face, you at one end,

me at the other, two minute
figures intent on their ascent,
into the shadows formed
between the sun-lit upper
roofs of rock, ourselves exultant and
glowing in the evening light, far above
the sheepwalk of the waiting ground.

For it seems to me that always,
even under grey and solid cloud,
our stalwart and quiet resolution
on the journey up, watching the rain
on the windscreen would earn its just
reward in weekend sun, the great
amphitheaters of rock become
our silent stage, long climbs following
the evening rays, step by lighted step,
into the upper shadows
of the coming night. For you
and I in my memory are forever
framed in sunlight, our newly youthful
hearts full of that impossible
and vertical world we
learned to call our own.

Now, putting down the phone,
looking east through the window,
over these once foreign, now
familiar, mountains toward you,
your voice receding into darkness
over six thousand miles of
land and turbulent water,

I feel you at a great
crossroads of movement, hesitant
only for a moment before
the new life
shaping before your eyes,
and I remember you intent,
eyes narrowed and searching,
watching the curve of the
cliff above you, one arm kept limp
beside your waist, saving its strength,
while the other holds you balanced.

Feet barely touching rock,
the black edge of your climbing
shoes smearing across
the airy nothing of a wafer ledge,
you tiptoe across the hanging
arch and disappear from view.

I watch the rope pay out into
sunlight and wreathed mist
and see your reappearance
in the columned roofs above.

The way you loved to work
slowly up a long groove
escaping through a daylight gap
barely visible below,
while I paid out slowly
the lengths of patient rope.

I watch you now
and mark your ascent
into this other
more difficult territory,
each step your own,

but me still careful
to watch you,
and your progress,
the rope
between us
like a living bond

and you thankfully
unaware, my brother,
intent on the passage
not seeing
(in the closeness of that
living earth)
the terrors of the
height to which you step.

DOUGIE

My uncle Dougie
was killed
on Sword Beach,
the 6th of June,
nineteen hundred
and forty four.

The cadence
of the date
like a slow chant
in my father's mind
round the one
central memory.

Dougie taught
him how to swim
before he died.

There are other words
still said
in unassuming
reverence
when our heads bend
over the letters
and you remake
and relive

the familiar loss,
as if forging his absence
new again,
each phrase measured
by its careful
placement in silence.

His regiment,
The East Yorkshires
I remember since
childhood and,
your Grandma and Grandpa
didn't know for months,
and now in final silence
the bleak
unnatural
and late arriving telegram
folded
and unfolded
down fifty years.

Sometimes I know
my father is
a young boy again
and Dougie,
teaching him how to swim,
has suddenly turned away
as if in a dream
and looks toward
France.

Then he is low down
in the water
near the horrific shore
and my father's arms
so recently taught
to live in that element
are reaching
to pull him back.

But the weighted surge
of his elder
brother's
pack and rifle

pull too much
for the young boy's arms.

Now I remember
my father's repeated
weekend need
for the ice cold waters
where he taught me
how to swim
and his fatherly
satisfaction
at the slowly
growing strokes
that kept his son
above water.

I could not know what
was being given then,
not knowing
how as the years pass
we must always strike
boldly to save those close to us,
hold them
above the drowning water
with our words,
so they live again,

if not the man,
then the loved
memory,

father to son,
brother to brother,
hand dipping in the water
toward shore,
saving them
now
as we could not then,
phrase by repeated phrase.

FIRELIGHT AND MEMORY

For Michael

The way the fire held in the grate
from day to day through that long winter,
you'd think the black coal was nestled
in the flames by invisible hands,
because in my memory we barely stirred
from talking. That year I came back
from the islands, the hearth blazed
through a whole winter of listening
and telling. You leaning forward
toward the warmth, hand raised
just like mine is now above the page
so your palm cupped and held
the glowing fire, and your forehead creased
with bearing down on the issue,
until you had it just right in your mind
and could feel it beginning to grow in mine.

Outside, the long valley of the Ogwen
was full of wind and bending trees,
night after November night in those cold rains
our minds grew numb to the outside sky
and we drew together for warmth
like the sheep huddled
in twos or threes about the farm,
hugging the walls and the frost scoured hollows.
Our faces were lit by the fire but our backs,
like theirs, were turned to the outside gale.
Inside, the talk fought hard against that dark,
the gales a constant backdrop
to our exploratory wintering blather.

That winter we spent together
in front of the endless fire,
everything we said seemed
necessary and important.
I see you still talking now,
looking back to me
over your shoulder
from the kitchen counter,
the teapot in your left hand
while the kettle bubbled
and steamed in your right,
carrying the point of the argument
through every movement,
until the final satisfying
set of the lid in the pot.

You wanted to know, you said,
if Blake was true in his meeting
with the angels or had exaggerated
an intuition to make the point we stand
in conversation with worlds
larger than ourselves. I loved the
youthful argument then,
but sense now, looking back,
haunting possibilities
to that final enquiry
so that affirmation or negation
of your repeated question
has enormous consequence
and you stand there
right across my past
as if blocking further access
to my future,

looking in me for a truth
I am not yet ready to know.

In that kitchen, you
still keep on talking,
and I, remembering you
year after year,
keep listening.

But then it was almost always
my enthusiastic talk
to your concentrated listening,
night after night, until
our November acquaintance eased
by January into firm friendship,
and I remember one midnight,
the exact moment we
first recognized a companionship
that remained solid for a lifetime,
laughing and raising
the winking glasses and in a delight at odds
with the shrieking through the trees,
we fell into a mutual discovery of lines
each of us had memorized alone,
our faces glowing equally with brandy,
bravo lines of Blake and the leaping fire.

We walked the hills in short bursts
between stinging showers, boiled
the few eggs the hens could muster
to an exact softness we thought
could bring a best beginning
and a rightness to the day.

We, with barely a hint of spring in that
sharp air, in the very cellar of winter
and snugged off from the tumult of the world,
were living out a summer of our friendship.
And I know now, like every other summer
in my northern memory, too short,
too much belonging to close affections,
too untouchable by the present,
and not recalled or remembered enough.

After that, just a few memories
more of you ghost through my mind,
like the sun's last rays passing over
the spread, red, bracken
of a Welsh September,
then right above the ridge
at Tan-y-Garth
I see your quick distant walking
silhouette, and you are gone.

I woke this morning
with those lit memories living
in my mind, and now
recalling you, the warmth
from that fire still heats my face
and has me look across
the empty grate to find you.
Your eyes half closed in concentration,
and your face raised, I see you
forever framed in firelight and now

I cannot tell if your serious angel
visits me through distant memory
or close proximity. You are there then,
in that time so utterly, that my present
seems stillborn, waiting, catching
its breath, for you to finish your sentence.
So strange that you should arrest me so,
your point always being that every corner
of creation sings its own aliveness
and speaks to us in tongues
we are afraid to learn.

Memory convinces me
you are as alive now as you were then,
me on this side, you on the other,
the fire now burning between us
the one that separates my life
from your death. This fire
lights my face on one side
and yours on the other
and I see my fear
at making a future transition
to your rested habitation
is a deep puzzle that frets you.
You want to know my fear
and you see in my face
a need for your persuasion.

I find the depth of our friendship
with you gone
has terrible consequences
and makes me think
of the possibilities of a life to come.
You make me long for a future
in which our past together
is still alive.

I put the pen to rest
on the table and turn
to hear
your imagined invitation
and by an empty grate,
trust again to your
companionship,

my idea of faith
this morning,
you and I by
some bright fire
snug
against the winter
of any past
or future
disappearance.

TRUE

Joel, God bless you,
you were wild
as a March Hare,
but brought
a spring scent
of fine revelation
to that troubled winter
I first met you.

I am thinking of the way
your talks were always
larger than their titles,
they were apprenticeships
to fate, dialogues with a destiny
always two steps ahead
of easy explanation.
On stage or at the table,
building a passionate theme,
you made it personal,
something we had left or neglected,
something we could
if we had the nerve,
touch again, you moved us
through insight or insult,
you trusted friendship
exactly because you were
careless of it and knew
the same robustness that
could break a bond,
could strengthen it,
deepen it, reinvent it
and bind those who felt it.

Joel, I think I love more
than anything
a real conversation—
I will miss you,
you were untamable by the world
in which you worked,
you stood at some frontier
we wanted for ourselves.
In my mind you stand there now
refusing to give up,
humorous but unbending,
engaging God to understand
the nature of his betrayal.

We allow it of you because
you always did trust
that dangerous edge in conversation,
the wild assertion, the sheer
hell with it nature of existence.
You didn't care, exactly because
you cared too much.

Your passion was our privilege.
You were a Whitman
of your world and
I salute you and thank you
in the style necessary
to your faith. I imagine
you here in your old way
looking over my shoulder
to make a summary,
a last line, by way of parting.
Something, wild,
ungovernable
and true.

LOOKING OUT FROM CLARE

For John O'Donohue

There's a great spring in you
all bud and blossom
and March laughter
I've always loved.

Your face framed
against the bay
and the whisper
of some arriving joke
playing at the mouth,
your lightning raid
on the eternal
melting the serious line
to absurdity.

I look round and see
the last days of winter
broken away
for all those
listening or watching,
all come to life now
with the first
pale sun on their face
for many a month,
remembering how to laugh.

But most of all I love
the heft and weight
and swing of that sea
behind it all, some other tide
racing toward the shore,
or receding to the calmness
where no light or laughter
lives for long.

The way you surface
from those atmospheres
again and again,
your emergence seems to make
you a lover of horizons
but your visitation
of darkness shows.

Then away from you,
I can see you only alone
on the strand,
walking to the sea
on the north shore of Clare
toward the end
of an unendurable winter,
as if taking your first swim
of the year.

The March scald
of cold ocean
even in May about to tighten
and bud you into spring.
You look across
the mountains in Connemara
framing, only for now,
your horizon.
You look and look, and look
beyond all looking.

RICHARD

For Philippa

When I open the door
you'll be standing there as solid
and as real as you always were,

the silhouette of the hills
you loved to walk
just behind your shoulder

and the corners of your mouth
playing the unspoken invitation
until you break into a smile.

And of course I'll come with you
walking and talking as we always did,
while the dusk and the dew

gather in the trees
until we reach the place
appointed by silence

where you have to go on
without me, to another
friendship, another invisible

marriage to which we both
apprenticed and to which
you recall me

when you turn
and look back
with the faith

I'll need to find you again.
Your face and hands
and words all farewell

and future invitation
behind you in the sky the star
I must follow

and the broad heaven
of my further
unfolding. Under this sky

you leave me shy again
and wondering,
remembering with what love

you came to me
at our first meeting
and our last parting.

Twice now, you
have made me a bride
to my future life.

THE FOX

For Doris Kareva

I remember the fox
and your train to the east,
two travellers, secret, and alone
in mutual recognition,
the eyes, the ears,
the wild red fur,
your look of surprise
at the sudden, tawny, flash
across the road,
knowing then, in the fox, the journey,
the way forward,
and our instincts already like him,
fugitive, glimpsed, already at bay,
you ready to stay or go
into what you loved,
your arrival in my life
so sudden and then
so quickly,
your final disappearance.

SUMMER READING

For Edward on his Fiftieth

There's winter
in a closed book,
a dormancy
of hidden words,
a pre-dawn impossibility
to the beckoning
image in the title.

With a new book
the crisp pages
are thin ice
cracking in springtime,
the clear current
of the story
just beginning to make
itself visible.

I love the birdsong
in a first line,
the wake-up
sense of stretching
on the right hand page,
the imperceptible
sense of
a new season breathed into
a landscape, a character,
a chapter,
things beginning to flit
from branch to branch,
the first lazy drift
of a bee toward the flowers

as the story opens
and suddenly
in the concentrated
listening,
the warm arc of the sun
is right on your neck,
as you sit in the garden
reading and receiving
the life giving rays,
arriving all the way
from far out
in the darkness, charged
and made benevolent
by the atmosphere of blue
and the shade of trees
and the birdsong
surrounding your concentration
on a story,
a dream, a drama,
a life come alive on the page,
your own intellect
and imagination
a kind of sunlight, a far out star
illuminating
from a great distance
the world you read,
making it sing,
making it new,
making it real,
making a summer
of a closed book.

[XVI]
ADMONITIONS

SELF-PORTRAIT

It doesn't interest me if there is one God
or many gods.
I want to know if you belong or feel
abandoned,
if you can know despair or see it in others.
I want to know
if you are prepared to live in the world
with its harsh need
to change you. If you can look back
with firm eyes,
saying this is where I stand. I want to know
if you know
how to melt into that fierce heat of living,
falling toward
the center of your longing. I want to know
if you are willing
to live, day by day, with the consequence of love
and the bitter
unwanted passion of your sure defeat.

I have heard, in *that* fierce embrace, even
the gods speak of God.

SWEET DARKNESS

When your eyes are tired
the world is tired also.

When your vision has gone,
no part of the world can find you.

Time to go into the dark
where the night has eyes
to recognize its own.

There you can be sure
you are not beyond love.

The dark will be your home
tonight.

The night will give you a horizon
further than you can see.

You must learn one thing.
The world was made to be free in.

Give up all the other worlds
except the one to which you belong.

Sometimes it takes darkness and the sweet
confinement of your aloneness
to learn

anything or anyone
that does not bring you alive

is too small for you.

ALL THE TRUE VOWS

All the true vows
are secret vows,
the ones we speak out loud
are the ones we break.

There is only one life
you can call your own
and a thousand others
you can call by any name you want.

Hold to the truth you make
every day with your own body,
don't turn your face away.

Hold to your own truth
at the center of the image
you were born with.

Those who do not understand
their destiny, will never understand
the friends they have made,
nor the work they have chosen,

nor the one life that waits
beyond all the others.

By the lake in the wood,
in the shadows,
you can
whisper that truth
to the quiet reflection
you see in the water.

Whatever you hear from
the water, remember,

it wants you to carry
the sound of its truth on your lips.

Remember,
in this place
no one can hear you

and out of the silence
you can make a promise
it will kill you to break,

that way you'll find
what is real and what is not.

I know what I am saying.
Time almost forsook me
and I looked again.

Seeing my reflection
I broke a promise
and spoke
for the first time
after all these years

in my own voice,

before it was too late
to turn my face again.

WHAT TO REMEMBER WHEN WAKING

In that first
hardly noticed
moment
in which you wake,
coming back
to this life
from the other
more secret,
moveable
and frighteningly
honest
world
where everything
began,
there is a small
opening
into the day
which closes
the moment
you begin
your plans.

What you can plan
is too small
for you to live.

What you can live
wholeheartedly
will make plans
enough
for the vitality
hidden in your sleep.

To be human
is to become visible,
while carrying
what is hidden
as a gift to others.

To remember
the other world
in this world
is to live in your
true inheritance.

You are not
a troubled guest
on this earth,
you are not
an accident
amidst other accidents,
you were invited
from another and greater
night
than the one
from which
you have just emerged.

Now, looking through
the slanting light
of the morning
window toward
the mountain
presence

of everything
that can be,
what urgency
calls you to your
one love? What shape
waits in the seed
of you to grow
and spread
its branches
against a future sky?

Is it waiting
in the fertile sea?
In the trees
beyond the house?
In the life
you can imagine
for yourself?
In the open
and lovely
white page
on the waiting desk?

THE JOURNEY

Above the mountains
    the geese turn into
      the light again

painting their
    black silhouettes
      on an open sky.

Sometimes everything
    has to be
      enscribed across
      the heavens

so you can find
    the one line
      already written
        inside you.

Sometimes it takes
    a great sky
      to find that

first, bright
    and indescribable
      wedge of freedom
        in your own heart.

Sometimes with
   the bones of the black
      sticks left when the fire
     has gone out

someone has written
   something new
    in the ashes
     of your life.

You are not leaving.
   Even as the light
    fades quickly now,
     you are arriving.

WORKING TOGETHER

We shape our self
to fit this world

and by the world
are shaped again.

The visible
and the invisible

working together
in common cause,

to produce
the miraculous.

I am thinking of the way
the intangible air

traveled at speed
round a shaped wing

easily
holds our weight.

So may we, in this life
trust

to those elements
we have yet to see

or imagine,
and look for the true

shape of our own self,
by forming it well

to the great
intangibles about us.

Written for the presentation of
The Collier Trophy to The Boeing Company
marking the introduction of the new 777 passenger jet.

LOAVES AND FISHES

This is not
the age of information.

This is *not*
the age of information.

Forget the news,
and the radio,
and the blurred screen.

This is the time
of loaves
and fishes.

People are hungry,
and one good word is bread
for a thousand.

THE NEW NOBILITY

The tawny gold of the first chantrelle
beneath the rough wall of fir bark,
a gleam in the undergrowth
to ignite the eye and ennoble the imagination.
Everyone is waiting for breakfast
to which I bring this husk and holiness
of the newly grown and the newly found.

White plates are laid along the table,
on each of them the omelettes
rest steaming, deep and rich,
the eggs brought from a friend's farm,
the chantrelles nested firmly
in their hot buttered interiors,
and the basil flecked
through them, plucked from the last
tangy stems of a summer garden.

Perfection is a fragile, ice-thin ground
that barely holds our human weight,
one false step and everything cracks
black to the edge. In this perfection,
no one dares mention the waters
of the Saratoga Passage shining through glass.
No one mentions our present happiness;
though the last dead century of grief
and misery has barely dropped from our grasp.

Outside the window, the children are playing
in borrowed clothes. One throws
back her head, sleeves trailing on the ground
and laughs in the sunlight,
and we laugh in witness, for in the midst of history
we are happy like them and all before them.
In their happiness everything still bears our weight.
Timelessness is the new nobility.

EVERYTHING IS WAITING FOR YOU

After Derek Mahon

Your great mistake is to act the drama
as if you were alone. As if life
were a progressive and cunning crime
with no witness to the tiny hidden
transgressions. To feel abandoned is to deny
the intimacy of your surroundings. Surely,
even you, at times, have felt the grand array;
the swelling presence, and the chorus, crowding
out your solo voice. You must note
the way the soap dish enables you,
or the window latch grants you freedom.
Alertness is the hidden discipline of familiarity.
The stairs are your mentor of things
to come, the doors have always been there
to frighten you and invite you,
and the tiny speaker in the phone
is your dream-ladder to divinity.

Put down the weight of your aloneness and ease into
the conversation. The kettle is singing
even as it pours you a drink, the cooking pots
have left their arrogant aloofness and
seen the good in you at last. All the birds
and creatures of the world are unutterably
themselves. Everything is waiting for you.

START CLOSE IN

Start close in,
don't take the second step
or the third,
start with the first
thing
close in,
the step
you don't want to take.

Start with
the ground
you know,
the pale ground
beneath your feet,
your own
way to begin
the conversation.

Start with your own
question,
give up on other
people's questions,
don't let them
smother something
simple.

To hear
another's voice,
follow
your own voice,
wait until
that voice

becomes a
private ear
that can
really listen
to another.

Start right now
take a small step
you can call your own
don't follow
someone else's
heroics, be humble
and focused,
start close in,
don't mistake
that other
for your own.

Start close in,
don't take
the second step
or the third,
start with the first
thing
close in,
the step
you don't want to take.

NO PATH

There is No Path that Goes all the Way
Han Shan

Not that it stops us looking
for the full continuation.

The one line in the poem
we can start and follow

straight to the end. The fixed belief
we can hold, facing a stranger

that saves us the trouble
of a real conversation.

But one day you are not
just imagining an empty chair

where your loved one sat.
You are not just telling a story

where the bridge is down
and there's nowhere to cross.

You are not just trying to pray
to a God you always imagined
would keep you safe.

No, you've come to a place
where nothing you've done

will impress and nothing you
can promise will avert

the silent confrontation,
the place where

your body already seems to know
the way, having kept

to the last, its own secret
reconnaissance.

But still, there is no path
that goes all the way,

one conversation leads
to another,

one breath to the next
until

there's no breath at all,

just
the inevitable
final release
of the burden.

And then,
wouldn't your life
have to start
all over again
for you to know
even a little
of who you had been?

INDEX OF POEM TITLES

A Woman's Voice 301
Actaeon Tells All..172
All the True Vows 347
Ancestral 112
Apology 167
Arrivals 75
At Home 9
Ayacucho 188

Bed Bugs in Kagbeni 300
Brendan 214

Coleman's Bed..288
Coming Back to the House 3
Cotswold 252
Cuzco 190

Dance Night in Waterford City 108
Death Waits 46
Dougie...321
Dreaming at Braga 299
Dun Aengus 283

Easter Morning in Wales..27
Edward...316
Everything is Waiting For You...359

Faith 94
Farewell Letter 104
Fire in the Earth...34
Firelight and Memory 325
First Steps in Hawkshead Churchyard.............................213
Fishing..99
Forgive..96
Four Horses 132

Hands Across the Water 265
Hartshead...254
Home 4

Horse in Landscape: Franz Marc 152
Horses Moving on the Snow 23
Huaras 186

In a Moment of Madness, a Dublin
   Poet Thinks of an Old Love 194
Inside 93
It Happens to Those Who Live Alone...12

John Clare's Madness 173

Kayak I..239
Kayak IV 240
Kayak VI...241

Learning To Walk 161
Light Over Water 24
Living Together 201
Loaves and Fishes 356
Looking 106
Looking out from Clare 334

Macchu Picchu 192
Mameen...286
Mariner 139
Marriage 202
Midsummer Prayer..48
Mortality My Mistress 67
Muktinath 293
Muse 122
My Daughter Asleep..217
My Poetry 137

Never Enough 178
New Year Prayer...180
News of Death...313
No One Told Me 131
No Path 362

Once Round the Moon..158
One Day 124

Open 44
Out On the Ocean 243
Owl Calls...26

Pisac, Peru 185
Poem in Praise of The Trinity Harp 271

Remember..165
Return..267
Revelation Must be Terrible 226
Richard 337

Second Birth 179
Seeking out Time..269
Seen from Above 28
Self -Portrait...345
Setting out at Dusk 246
Seven Steps for Coming Home 121
Sitting Zen...43
Sligo Glen: Walking out of Silence 59
Sometimes 52
Song For the Salmon 146
Spiddal Harbour 1976 268
Start Close In...360
Statue of Buddha 308
Statue of Shiva 309
Stepping Stones 114
Summer Reading..340
Sweet Darkness 346

Tan-y-Garth...314
Takstang...303
Tempus Omnia Revelat 117
Ten Years Later 247
The All of It...281
The Bell Ringer..62
The Body in Full Presence 130
The Faces at Braga 296
The Fire in the Song 228
The Fox..339
The Half Turn of Your Face 50

The Hawthorn 195
The Hazel Wood 78
The Horse Whisperer 273
The House of Belonging 6
The Journey 352
The Lightest Touch 136
The New Nobility 357
The Old Interior Angel 305
The Opening of Eyes 31
The Painter's Hand 125
The Poet 128
The Poet as Husband 204
The Seven Streams 285
The Shell 101
The Song of the Lark 32
The Soul Lives Contented 225
The Sound of the Wild 230
The Task at Hand 123
The Thicket 56
The Truelove 198
The Vows at Glencolmcille 205
The Well of Grief 95
The Well of Stars 155
The Wildflower *25*
The Winter of Listening 16
There are Those 251
This Poem a Prayer Flag 302
This Poem Belongs to You 135
This Time 175
Threshold 97
Tiananmen 276
Tilicho Lake 295
Time Left Alone 149
Tobar Phadraic 287
Traveling to London 35
True 331

Unutterable Name 38
Up On the Hill's Back 33

Vision on the Hills 147

Waiting to Go On 70
Watching the Sun Go Down 245
We Shall Not be Here 45
What is it Like? 171
What it Means to be Free 151
What to Remember When Waking 349
When the Wind Flows 54
Where Many Rivers Meet 145
Who Made The Stars? 81
Winter Child 15
Working Together..354

You Darkness 154
Yorkshire 256

INDEX OF FIRST LINES

A cold wind off the mountain 188

A garden inside me, unknown, secret 27

A sandstone grave crowding shellfish 252

Above the mountains 352

All the true vows 347

All the water below me came from above 145

An open sandy shell 101

As I sit here writing 123

At home amidst 9

And then, after 59

And we know, when Moses was told 34

And when you go, try to go before Easter 283

After her death, I sat by the river 99

After three days of sitting 43

Aquiline, yet youthful, resembling 316

Be infinitesimal under that sky, a creature 286

Blue lights on the runway like stars 155

Carrying a child 217

Cold morning on a strange bed 300

Coleridge's eyes 35

Come down drenched, at the end of May 285

Coming back to the house I lean down into the snow 3

Consider the bell 62

Cross-currents and tumbling desire 38

Dawn at Muktinath 293

Death waits behind the branches 46

Far up and off.. 112

For too many days now I have not written of the sea 146

Finally 230

From the northeast.. 240

Good poetry begins with 136

Heaven has been 45

Home 4

I awoke 6
I arrived at last, five hours before she died 96
I lay a handful of walnuts 70
I love the dead 256
I remember the fox... 339
I remember those trees along the along the water...................... 185
I saw a stag through the mist, silver.. 172
I was always half-asleep 114
I want to write about faith 94
I write in a small shadowed corner 204
Imagine the confines of a long grey corridor 75
Impossible to write about Ireland 265
In Hartshead I'm walking paths I've walked for years 254
In Ireland, Time has never been understood.............................269
In midsummer, under the luminous 48
In monastery darkness 296
In that first 349
In the evening, that shadow on Coldspring................................ 245
In the center of this wildflower 25
In these waves... 243
In this high place 295
In winter 23
Inside this sitting here... 93
Ireland's the ghost-horse 272
It became clear 190
It doesn't interest me if there is one God 345
It happens to those 12
It is a small step to remember.. 44
It is never enough. The three riders 178
It is night...268
It's as if the solid 205

Joel, God bless you 331
Jupiter in the western sky 214

Last night they came with news of death 313
Late evening in Esthwaite and the half-moon rides.................... 26

Make a nesting now, a place to which....................................... 288
Moves forward 128
My mother is a young girl again... 106

My poetry is all 137
My son strode out into the world today 213
My uncle Dougie 321
Myself at my door 15

Night at Latamarang 301
No one but me by the fire 16
No one told me 131
Northamptonshire's 173
Now I know my great success 167

One step to take notice 121
On the way from Kenmare 276
On Thursday the farmer 132
Once round the moon 158
One day I will 124

Revelation must be 226
Rough barked, walnut brown, milky darkness 271

Seeing from a high window 28
She wrote me a letter 104
Silence 67
So many years since I saw you last 165
Sometimes 52
Sometimes it is like this; a crowded 78
Start close in 360
Surrounded by stones and trees 139

Takstang monastery 303
Two miles to go and the door will open 299
That day I saw beneath dark clouds 31
That full view of the world seen as a child 147
The body in full presence 130
The crossed knot 195
The day started with a flurry of gulls 267
The gold hands of the clock 117
The half turn of your face 50
The kayak 239
The kayak sits on the black water 246
The mouth opens 228

The standing stones are silent, the ground will not speak 149
The song begins and the eyes are lifted 32
The soul lives contended 225
The tangle of it all, the briar curve perspective 56
The tawny gold of the first chantrelle 357
The way the fire held in the grate 325
The wild dream, two whirling lights 179
The words insistent, wishing to be said 122
There are those we know 251
There is a faith in loving fiercely 198
There were words in the end 97
There's a great spring in you 334
There's winter 340
This book-lined perspective 281
This grass-grown hill's a patchwork lined with walls 314
There is No Path that Goes all the Way 362
This is not 356
This poem 135
This poem a prayer flag 302
This robust heart involved 180
This sense of looking down 192
This skin I should shed 202
This time he has gone 175
Those mountains out of my past 186
Those who will not slip beneath 95
Through the light on the upper line of water 24
Turn sideways into the light as they say 287
Twenty years since I knew her 194

Up on the hill's back 33

Walked out this morning 161
We know the fiery animality 152
We shape our self 354
We sit on the plane, we watch 151
We are like children in the master's violin shop 201
What is it like to be alone? 171
When I open the door 337
When the mind is clear 247
When the mind lets go at last 241
When the wind flows 54

When you had that dream 108
When your eyes are tired 346
Who made the stars? 81

You darkness from which I come 154
You start... 125
Young, male and.. 305
Your great mistake is to act the drama 359
Your hand moves 308

For more information about books and recordings;
seminars, retreats or speaking engagements
by David Whyte
please contact:

Many Rivers Company
P.O. Box 868
Langley, WA 98260
(360) 221-1324
www.davidwhyte.com

David Whyte makes his home in the Pacific
Northwest, where rain and changeable skies
remind him of his other, more distant homes:
Yorkshire, Wales and Ireland. He travels and
lectures throughout North America, Europe,
South Africa and Asia, bringing his own and
others' poetry to large audiences. He is one of the
few poets to bring his insights to bear on
organizational life, working with companies at
home and abroad.